#EmbraceTheDetour

#EmbraceTheDetour

The Entrepreneur Detour

WHAT THEY CAN'T TEACH YOU
IN BUSINESS SCHOOL

Kevin Cortez

3

The Entrepreneur Detour: What They Can't Teach You in Business School

Published by: ENTRUST, Dallas, TX USA

Copyright © 2017, 2023 Kevin Cortez

Paperback ISBN: 978-0-692-86198-1

Ebook ISBN: 069286198X

For ordering information or special discounts, please contact *Kevin Cortez Media* at 800-858-8507.

Published in the United States of America

Library of Congress Cataloging in Publication Data

Name: Cortez, Kevin

Title: The Entrepreneur Detour: What They Can't Teach You in Business School by Kevin Cortez

Categories: BUS025000 BUSINESS / Entrepreneurship and BUS043000 BUSINESS / Marketing / General

Second Edition

This page is supposed to be
Praise for the Book
by famous people.

Hey, I just want to say *thank you*! I really appreciate you taking the time to check this book out.

Typically, this endorsement page targets people considering if they will purchase *The Entrepreneur Detour*. This page is designed to help you realize how awesome this book is.

Preferably, the accolades are written by famous people whom everybody respects. Then, hopefully, you will be impressed enough to buy it.

As much as I would like to have those endorsements, I would instead use this page to encourage those of you considering purchasing this book to check out the customer reviews on Amazon. Those are real people who have actually taken the time and put forth the extra effort to make their thoughts known.

I genuinely believe "the market" will reflect its value—or not.

– Kevin

P.S. It would mean the world to me to have your feedback (even if it's not five stars). I promise I will read *every* review with appreciation.

Contents

With Gratitude

To my parents, Don and Jody Cortez. Words cannot do justice to the level of gratitude I feel for them. The older I get, the more I appreciate my growing up in their household. What an incredible gift I received.

And also to my grandparents, Joe and Thelma McNally. In 1946, they risked everything to establish a business that has helped our family for generations. I am part of their legacy, and this book is a tribute to who they were.

Introduction

I live in one of the fastest-growing cities in the country: Frisco, Texas. It has become a magnet for companies investing billions of dollars into development. Even one of the world's most valuable sports organizations, the Dallas Cowboys football team, has moved its world headquarters and training facilities to this suburb of Dallas. Go Cowboys!

Because of construction in Frisco, traffic is absolutely crazy! Our area is growing so fast that even Google Maps has difficulty keeping up with the day-to-day road detours. Do you know what this means?

Many times, my GPS directions are not accurate. In fact, sometimes, the route Mr. Google tells me to take is flat-out wrong. Driving anywhere in North Dallas has become unpredictable at best.

Not too long ago, I jumped into my car, turned on my Maps app to route me to an address, and started driving. I knew there was a major construction delay ahead, and if I followed Google's directions, it would take me much longer to reach my destination. Naturally, I was not in the mood to sit in my car longer than necessary.

The voice from my phone kept telling me, "You are on the fastest route," but I had some personal information that said otherwise. A detour I was aware of would get me to my destination much quicker, so I went that way. My GPS kept trying to reroute me and telling me to turn around. Finally, I just turned the app off and continued on my detour.

As I drove, I realized that what I was experiencing related very well to entrepreneurship, and that moment became the genesis of this book.

The more I thought about it, the more I realized how the entrepreneurial life is a rough road, replete with potholes and detours.

I don't know about you, but I have a terrible sense of direction. That's why I find it so remarkable when I jump into my car, speak the words "OK, Google" into my Android smartphone (sorry iPhone users), then say an address or business name, tap "DIRECTIONS," and just like magic, a voice from Google Maps directs me to my destination.

It is so much better than fumbling through a *Rand McNally Road Atlas*. Do you remember those things? Sheesh, what a pain!

Before using the GPS navigation on my mobile phone, I constantly pulled over to figure out where I was. As I drove around Dallas using an outdated map I could never fold back up correctly, traffic updates on the radio became mission-critical. We have it so much better today!

How does all this correlate to being an entrepreneur? When we jump into our cars, we plan to go *somewhere*. And we usually know how we plan to get to our destination: which roads to take, what times are best to avoid rush-hour traffic, and how weather factors into our journey. We also know that sometimes we'll run into a detour. As we are driving, we encounter something we didn't plan on, and it causes us to make a U-turn or go down a street we did not expect to take.

If you are an entrepreneur, you have a destination. Everyone who's ever had an idea for a business has a place they want their business to arrive at. They begin their journey to that destination, but almost immediately they encounter a steady stream of detours. Then, as time grinds on, they can become frustrated with the process and begin to question *everything*.

Can you relate?

There is a better way to live as an entrepreneur, but it will involve going against the grain and not following conventional wisdom. In fact, you will be forced into taking some unconventional detours if you are to succeed in the current business climate.

EMBRACE THE DETOUR

I assume you wouldn't be reading this book if you weren't interested in entrepreneurship. You may aspire to be an entrepreneur, or you may already be a full-fledged, successful business owner. Either way, I hope to encourage you to keep going and warn you of potential hazards on the road ahead.

Does your current road look like the one you envisioned for your business at the start of your adventure? I doubt it.

Has the progress of your journey slowed down or stalled? Most likely.

Or worse, do you feel like the path you're actually on is taking you in the wrong direction?

If that's you, welcome to *The Entrepreneur Detour*.

Most detours are unexpected and usually inconvenient. This messes with our emotions.
We become impatient.
We complain.
We become confused.
We struggle.
We wonder why in the world did this happen to us right now.

Here's the good news: entrepreneur detours can actually be good events that often feel bad ... and they can end up being very positive moments for you and your business. Just make sure you're responding to them correctly.

"Entrepreneur detours can actually be good events that often feel bad."

@realKevinCortez #EmbraceTheDetour

As veteran entrepreneurs know all too well, making the right decisions is usually hard and can feel extremely uncomfortable. But, if you aren't careful and react incorrectly, your situation could go from bad to worse— to a lot worse. This is one of the many reasons so many businesses fail.

I will be the first to admit that every entrepreneurial experience is as unique as the person having it. Business ownership is very personal. *The Entrepreneur Detour* will take you to unexpected places you never planned for.

There is a ton of information available detailing how to be a Rock-Star Entrepreneur. That is why I didn't write a "how-to" book. I will leave many of those tactics to those who are much smarter than me. Besides, I would never pretend to have all the answers.

Rather than waste your time repeating advice already out there, I will help you create better questions for where you are on your entrepreneurial journey—questions specifically applicable to your situation. Then you will have a framework to arrive at your own answers (making what you read relevant to you personally).

> ## "Ask better questions to make better decisions."
> @realKevinCortez #EmbraceTheDetour

I'd much rather make sure you understand the context and implications that go with being an entrepreneur than tell you what to do in your entrepreneurial journey. My goal is to lay out some of the unchanging truths about what every entrepreneur has gone through, is presently going through, or is about to go through.

I hope my story, with all its twists and turns, will simply bring another perspective to those interested in entrepreneurship. My driving force for documenting some of the unpredictable events I've encountered in my life is to have what I've shared help you win.

Life, in general, is messy, unpredictable, and pretty amazing. Entrepreneur life is all those things times fifty. Do you feel as though no one else is going through the same things as you? You'd be surprised to see how normal your crazy entrepreneurial life really is. When I've detailed parts of my story with others in an unvarnished way, a common response is, "Hearing about what you've experienced makes me feel normal."

I'm here to hopefully impart some wisdom and understanding so you will know how to make better decisions as your journey unfolds. What I've gone through will demonstrate that you can be on the right road even when life seems to be going all wrong.

Despite the obstacles that await us all, I believe we are living in the greatest era in human history to be an entrepreneur.

The barriers to entry for business have come crashing down because of technology and automation.

The playing field has been leveled.

The market awaits.

So, together, let's *#EmbraceTheDetour*.

CHAPTER 1

The Journey
of an Entrepreneur

In May of 1983, I was preparing to graduate from California Polytechnic State University in San Luis Obispo. In a few weeks, my life would transition into the real world. For the first time since I was five years old, I would not be going to school in the fall.

I'd planned to spend the summer with my friend Alan Meyers, who lived in London and then work somewhere fun for a year before getting a real job. That meant I could enjoy my last few months of freedom in Europe and then move to Hawaii so I could goof off for a year. That plan was my graduation gift to myself.

I had it all figured out: since I was a Certified United States Tennis Academy Teaching Professional and a Black Belt Karate Instructor, I'd teach tennis during the day at a nice resort, and at night, I'd teach karate. I thought working at a resort would help in my pursuit of one day owning a health club, and teaching karate would give me extra cash because I knew the cost of living in Hawaii was high.

A DEFINING MOMENT

On May 17, while lying in bed in my college apartment, my plans for my immediate future dramatically changed. I woke up to the voice of Ruth Carter Stapleton, the sister of former president Jimmy Carter, being interviewed on a TV show. She was talking about her battle with pancreatic cancer and how the doctors had given her only a few months to live.

What captured me was that this unbelievable lady was at total peace with her situation. I wondered, "How in the world can this woman handle what she's going through with such courage and grace?" Suddenly, touring Europe for the summer and spending a year improving the tennis game of pretty ladies in a tropical paradise seemed selfish and small-minded.

Lying there in bed, I had a radical conversation with myself. Allow me to share a bit of my journal. Some of the thoughts I had were:

To be or not to be? That is not the question.
(Where in the world did that thought come from?)
Am I going to be the kind of person God created me to be? That is the question.

I thought about how I wanted to be the type of person that is a positive influence in the lives of others. What if I went ahead and went to London but didn't go to Hawaii? What would I do instead? Hmm.

What if I spent that year focusing on actually learning how to become a better person instead of having fun? Interesting.

What would that look like? How would I pull that off? I haven't a clue.

How would developing strong character in my life really benefit me?

Remember, this was the early 1980s—before self-help icon Tony Robbins and the personal development movement had taken hold of our culture. This was before everybody ran around quoting the German philosopher Frederick Nietzsche (not my favorite thinker, but even those we don't like can come up with wise thoughts), who once said, "He who has a *why* to live for can bear almost any *how*" (emphasis added).[1] Our "why" is the thing that motivates us to get up every morning and work a little harder to get a little better.

Most people know how to focus on *what* they have to do. Some people know *how* they need to do it. But very few people understand *why* they do what they do.

Do you know what the thing is that has the ability to push you even on the days when all you want to do is pull the covers over your head and retreat from the world?

"What has the ability to push you?"

@realKevinCortez #EmbraceTheDetour

At twenty-three, I sure didn't know my *why*. I had no idea what purpose, cause, or belief inspired me to do anything. I didn't know what it was I really wanted to do and who it was I wanted to be. I just knew that if I started moving in a direction that might provide some answers, I would hopefully figure things out as I went.

On May 17, 1983, I completely adjusted my future. That decision was reinforced in my mind four months later when Ms. Carter died. To this day, it still fascinates me how one person's courage can alter someone else's life in less than five minutes.

After my summer in England (Thank you, Alan), I packed everything I owned into my 1976 Chevrolet Monza 2+2 hatchback and moved from California to Dallas, Texas. I planned to attend a Leadership and Bible Institute for one year and then decide what to do next. You can judge me. It's cool. That's the only thing I could think of at the time. (Whoops, I ended up going back to school after all!)

This was the first major decision I'd ever made in my life that was not based on what others thought I should do. Understandably, this didn't go over too well with my mom and dad, but they supported my decision just like they had always done. Oh man, I won the lottery having them as my parents!

While all my friends were advancing in their chosen careers, I was studying such subjects as *Practical Christian Living*, *Leadership*, *Issues of the Heart*, and *Character Development*. When I would talk to my buddies, they'd tell me about the new cars they were driving and the nice places they were living. That wasn't my reality. I was learning about *Wisdom and Guidance*, *Financial Stewardship*, *The Disciplined Life*, and *Interpersonal Relationships*.

I'll admit: talking to my friends stung a bit, especially since I was making $4.50 an hour and eating ninety-nine-cent tacos at Jack in the Box every other day. (That's one unhealthy way to lose twenty pounds). But I believed my actions would help me in the long run. What started out as my one-year experiment to better understand myself and life in general turned into eight years.

As I look back, I can honestly say that giving up most of my twenties to focus on understanding why my life unfolded in the way it had, not to mention increasing my self-awareness, has been one of the best decisions I've ever made. On the surface, it looked like I was falling behind others my age. But it has become a tremendous advantage in several areas of my life, including professionally.

FAILURE IS REAL

To keep up with my classes, work, and personal life in Dallas, I put together a small three-ring binder with sections to organize everything. This binder became my first real business venture. I called it the "Overcomers Organizer." It was divided into seven sections, each designed to complement the other. It was my "personal blueprint for success and achievement." Do you like the nice tagline I came up with?

This planner was actually the first Christian organizer that involved integrating a person's faith into goal-setting, daily planning, and journaling that I'm aware of being brought to market. From what I can tell, it was a precursor to the Franklin Planner system published that following year.

While preparing to pull together my first small batch of binders to sell, I shared my business idea with a fast-talking media guy named Bob. He was one of those dudes who was constantly bouncing from thought to thought, daring you to keep up. He'd been hired to fill a national Christmas gift catalog with products. Bob told me he would feature my planner in that catalog. I only had to produce a large quantity of organizers before the catalog was released to the public. Why? "So, we'll have the inventory on hand when all those people rush to order your organizer," he said.

I was super pumped, but there was one problem: I had no money to do what Bob said needed to be done. I'd gotten a raise at work to six dollars an hour, but that wasn't enough to help me "go big." The only place I could think of that had that kind of money was a bank.

So, I scheduled an appointment with a bank president I'd met a few months earlier named Wendell. As I sat in his beautiful office, I asked him if he had any advice. He liked me and my business idea so much that he gave me a commercial loan to finance the entire project. Wendell said he would personally sign off on the loan, especially since the planner was going to be featured in a prominent catalog in a few months.

I became a *real* entrepreneur that day. Little did I know what kind of an adventure I was in for. I experienced the highest high the day the truck pulled up to the front of my duplex and dropped off pallets of my *Overcomers Organizer*. But that feeling was short-lived.

A few days later, I called Bob to let him know I now had the inventory in stock and everything was set on my end. He said not to worry about that because he had changed his mind and decided to put a pretty necklace in my spot in the gift catalog.

So much for someone's word being their bond. Note-to-younger-self: *get things like this in writing in the future.*

Being an entrepreneur is great—except when it's not. In one gut-wrenching moment, my highest emotional high was replaced with a devastating new low. That was my welcome to entrepreneurship: a jump-spinning kick to the teeth.

Failure is real—The bruises of that defeat would linger for years.

"Being an entrepreneur is great—except when it's not."

@realKevinCortez #EmbraceTheDetour

I sold several of those organizers, but sales were not even remotely close to what I needed in light of my on-hand inventory versus the outstanding commercial loan I was responsible for. Thankfully, after several extremely stressful months, I was able to sell all of my remaining organizers to a wonderful man in New Mexico who loved the planner. I sold them, along with the publishing rights, at cost. This was the first of many entrepreneurial detours I'd experience over the years.

Interesting fact: I now see a very similar planner was launched in 2015, and it looks like it's become a big success. I guess I was just thirty years too early.

THE MARKET DOESN'T CARE

Part of enjoying your entrepreneurial journey is understanding that detours are inevitable. Far too often, we fail to understand our detours and, as a result, we wind up viewing them with the wrong perspective. All entrepreneurs experience setbacks, failures, letdowns, and obstacles.

How can we tell if we're correctly looking at detours? Easy. When we experience impatience, bitterness, regret, or doubt, we need to adjust our focus. Rather than allowing the detours to show us what lessons need to be learned or what opportunities the detour may have created, we allow all that is wrong to consume our thoughts. This hinders our progress and sets us back, sometimes permanently.

When we don't grasp what we need to learn from leaving the main route, more detours are required to get us to our destination. It can become a vicious cycle. Have you ever had your GPS keep rerouting you, and it seemed like you were going in circles? It's like that.

For example, I looked at my *Overcomers Organizer* experience as a test. The whole thing let me know where I stood in the world of being an entrepreneur. It identified some things I needed to learn and some skill sets I needed to develop—like don't ever believe a fast-talking man named Bob. Since I didn't pass that particular test, I obviously needed to adjust my perspective so that when the next test (opportunity) came my way, I'd have some clarity on what decisions I should make so I could pass it.

Some people may be able to "test out" of an entrepreneurial class because they have what it takes to pass the exam. They have enough experience to skip the rest of the assignment. We all know people who are just plain gifted and seem to make things look easy. (Don't you just hate people like that? Kidding.) Unfortunately, most of us have to go through the learning process—some of us more often than others—in order to gain what is needed to move our businesses forward.

Whether through uncontrollable circumstances or the consequences of wrong choices, everyone has experienced unforeseen changes in life. Are you at the place you want to be on your entrepreneurial journey?

If not, are you making excuses so you don't have to make necessary changes? Please realize you probably have much more control than you think. It may not feel like it, but you do.

The market is only interested in making money. Does the market care about you and your challenges? In French: non. In Spanish: no. In English: nope. In German: nein. The sooner you realize that the market isn't interested in making the process easy for you, the sooner you will start doing what you know you have to do. Actually, the best way to think about it is: the market is the decision-maker; the Internet is the gatekeeper.

> "The market is only interested in making money."
>
> @realKevinCortez #EmbraceTheDetour

THE SHIFT

Are you familiar with the term *gatekeeper*? If you were to Google "how to get past the gatekeeper," you would find around 2,680,000 results. If you've had any form of sales training, you will undoubtedly have had training on how to get past the person (gatekeeper) responsible for people gaining access to the decision-maker. Typically, this is a personal assistant or a secretary, but in some companies it can be the receptionist or person answering the phones.

If you were an entrepreneur before social media networks, you were at the mercy of the Gatekeeper. This middleman had absolute control. But now, thanks to technology, the Internet is the middleman, and we have way more control than we used to. We can directly engage with the market through social engagement and digital marketing. That is a massive shift from how things used to be. Today, with your smartphone, laptop, and Internet connection, you can win.

Think about it: Where is everyone's attention being directed these days? Generally speaking, it's the Internet. Or, more specifically, our smartphones.

It's crazy for me to think that around eight-in-ten Americans use social media to connect with one another, engage with news content, share information, shop, and entertain themselves.[2] And it's not slowing down, as more and more people are adopting this behavior every single day.

Since the Internet is where our attention is, don't you think it's essential to have an effective marketing strategy that takes this into account? For me, that was an extremely difficult detour to take. I had to acknowledge that my twenty-plus years of traditional broadcast marketing experience was no longer as relevant as it once was. Here's the unalterable truth: the market *is* the market. I had to let go of my ego and learn an entirely different way of marketing and brand development. Ugh.

As you read the following pages, my hope is that you are encouraged to see how I handled some things that flipped my world on its head. Learn from my setbacks so you too can move forward, avoid some of my mistakes, and *#EmbraceTheDetour*!

Chapter Reflections

What are your thoughts? I would love for you to share some of your answers to these questions on any of my social media platforms. Go to "KevinCortez.com" and link to them from there.

1. I spent most of my twenties focusing on increasing my self-awareness. Have you spent any focused time trying to figure out why your life unfolds the way it does?
2. What is your *why*? What has the ability to push you?
3. As you consider your entrepreneurial journey, how have you been affected by the unexpected challenges that showed up?

Scan the QR Code for bonus content.

CHAPTER 2

The Definition
of an Entrepreneur

For some unknown reason, I've always been attracted to business. I grew up during the 1960s and 1970s, and the term *entrepreneur* wasn't common back then. I wasn't sure what it meant to others, but when I first heard someone was an entrepreneur, I thought it just meant they had some good ideas but weren't necessarily a *real* businessperson.

I was raised in the working-class neighborhood of the small town of Bishop, California. My father, Don, worked at the phone company. My mother, Jody, was a teacher at the elementary school located just two streets over from the house I grew up in.

Bishop is an isolated town situated in the Owens Valley, one of the two valleys in the contiguous United States with mountain ranges over fourteen thousand feet on either side. Bishop is 250 miles northeast of Los Angeles and is part of the Eastern Sierra outdoor recreational area, famous for snow skiing, sport climbing, mountain biking, horseback riding, and great fishing in nearby mountain lakes and streams. People in Southern California would save all year long just to vacation in an area I lived in every day.

There was a neighbor boy I admired who lived four houses down from me. Robbie was my age, and he was a kid-businessman. He had a newspaper route; I thought that was the coolest thing.

The way I remember, I thought it was amazing that he actually got paid to ride his bicycle. In fact, I thought it was so great that I would ride my Schwinn bike with him and help him throw those papers every chance I got. I didn't care about getting paid or not. Even at a young age, I just loved the idea of "working."

Then, as luck would have it, when Robbie's parents took him on vacation, the only one who knew which houses got papers on his route was me. Score! My first business transaction! This highlights my favorite definition of *luck,* commonly attributed to the Roman philosopher Seneca: "Luck is when opportunity meets preparation."

You should have seen how proud I was to be the one responsible for throwing those papers all by myself. I turned it into a game and would try to get those products as close to the front doors as possible. To this day, it irks me when I see a newspaper at the edge of a driveway— such poor customer service.

For those of you baby boomers or older, you ought to remember that when we grew up, "work" was considered a positive thing. I don't believe the bestselling book, *The*

4-Hour Workweek would have been nearly as popular back then as it is today.

I am so thankful that those odd jobs I did in my early childhood laid the foundation for a work ethic I still build on to this day. Riding my bike after school to Spoor's Sheet Metal Shop to sweep the floors with my classmate Jeff gave me a strong sense of accomplishment. And I thoroughly enjoyed painting fences at the Sportsman Inn Motel with my friend Clay, the owner's son.

LESSON LEARNED

Then, the summer before my first year of high school, it happened. I landed the most coveted summer job (in my mind) any teenager could get in Bishop: working as a gas station attendant at Tony's 76. Yes, there was a time when all gas stations were full-service. Now, only those living in Oregon and New Jersey know the joy of not having to get out of your car to fill your own gas tank (since it's illegal to do so).

Granted, the general manager of the gas station owed my father a favor because Dad had gotten the manager's son a job at the phone company. Whatever the cause, I got to spend forty hours every week pumping gas, washing windshields, and checking oil with some very popular Bishop High upperclassmen. I had the privilege of working at Tony's every summer during my high school years, which enabled me to save the money I needed to apply toward my upcoming college experience.

I learned many valuable life lessons over those summers, but one will always stand out. I can still clearly remember it.

I dropped by the station on a Sunday afternoon to check the schedule to see what hours I'd be working over the next two-week period. To my utter dismay, my name was no longer on the schedule.

I went into the owner's office to point out the obvious oversight. That's when Mr. Johnson taught me a powerful lesson I'll never forget. As I recall, Mr. Johnson said, "I've seen that you've been sick on one day each of the last several weeks."

Oops. Busted!

Mr. Johnson then told me, "Since you like having time off to do other things with your friends, you can have some extra time off to have fun with your buddies."

He finished by telling me to "think about if you really want to work here and let me know your decision after the two weeks are up."

Whew! Good thing Mr. Johnson had been friends with my father since high school, or I may have had to look for another job. What do you think I did? Let's just say *lesson learned*. After this experience, I never took any job for granted. It got my attention, and over the next four summers, I don't recall ever calling in sick again.

Although I'm bummed I missed out on such cool things as Big Wheels and Polyurethane Skateboard Wheels, I am so thankful I grew up during a time where real skills, proven character, and meritocracy were emphasized—a time when privilege, status, and influence were earned and not simply passed down. What an incredible gift that was.

Over the years, I have become a defender of all things entrepreneurial. As such, I have also developed a deep appreciation for entrepreneurs! I'm not talking about the wannabe visionaries who dream about making a killing in an IPO and have books written about them. I'm referring to entrepreneurs in the old-fashioned sense, who start a business to provide a better life for themselves and their families.

ENTREPRENEURS ARE MY HEROES

I love hanging around entrepreneurs who put their careers and savings at risk every day. They don't have a fallback plan and certainly aren't counting on the next funding round for their overhyped startup. The veteran entrepreneurs I'm talking about have gone through phenomenal wars and have the battle scars and dents in their armor to prove it.

In general, people with bright, shiny armor make me nervous. It's a safe bet that they don't know how to go through anything because they haven't gone through anything. Let's just say I wouldn't want them watching my back in the heat of battle.

Do you know what it's like to face down real failure, the kind that comes with personal bankruptcy? Entrepreneurs live with this possibility every day.

It's a constant challenge to define what an entrepreneur is. When I recently looked up the word *entrepreneur* online, Wikipedia said:

> *Traditionally, an entrepreneur has been defined as a person who starts, organizes, and manages any enterprise, especially a business, usually with considerable initiative and risk. Rather than working as an employee, an entrepreneur runs a small*

business and assumes all the risk and reward of a given business venture, idea, or good or service offered for sale.

The entrepreneur is commonly seen as a business leader and innovator of new ideas and business processes.

Entrepreneurs tend to be good at perceiving new business opportunities. They often exhibit positive biases in their perception (i.e., a bias towards finding new possibilities and seeing unmet market needs) and a pro-risk-taking attitude that makes them more likely to exploit the opportunity.[3]

Entrepreneurship is in my blood. My grandfather, Joe McNally, cashed out his cattle-ranching business and went into partnership with a gentleman named Bob Kelso in 1946. Mr. Kelso had founded Eastern Sierra Wholesalers a few years previously and began distributing various products throughout the area. They worked together for a few years until my grandfather bought Mr. Kelso out.

I have wonderful childhood memories of running around the original warehouse of this wholesale distribution company, playing on the pallets of beer and picking out all kinds of candy from the storage racks in one of the back corners of the facility.

My grandfather definitely fit the definition of an entrepreneur. He had to put forth considerable initiative and assumed all the risk as he established our family business from the late 1940s into the early 1960s.

He was incredibly good at perceiving new business opportunities and expanding the beer, wine, and liquor product categories his company sold to retailers. He became one of the prominent business leaders in the two central California counties of Inyo and Mono.

Unfortunately, Grandpa Joe died unexpectedly in 1962 at the young age of forty-eight. Since I was only two years old at the time, I don't remember him, but I grew up hearing some touching stories. This beloved man left a legacy through the positive difference he made in so many lives. Those stories of his generosity and kindness continue to have a tremendous impact on me to this very day.

WORK HARD AND SAVE YOUR MONEY

After my grandfather passed away, my wonderful Grandma Thelma ran our family business until my father left his secure job at the Continental Telephone Company to take over the reins in the early 1970s.

Looking back, without question, my dad has been the person most responsible for teaching me the value of work. His example has always inspired me. He definitely instilled in me those things that are absolutely critical to being successful in any business endeavor.

For example, I wanted a minibike so badly when I was young! The moment Jeff Plank let me ride his Honda 50 when I was eight years old, I was hooked. I didn't even care when I crashed. I still have a scar from the foot peg that punctured my ankle after one such crash. (It was worth it). I remember feeling absolute freedom as I rode that dirt bike.

My dad told me he would pay for half of a minibike if I saved up the other half. It took me almost three years to save that $167, but I did it. I would pocket every penny that came my way. Dad walking me out to the garage when I was eleven years old to show me my brand-new Yamaha 60 is still one of the most exciting days of my life.

Hopefully, I'm expressing clearly what I believe with all my heart: If you're an entrepreneur, you had better know the importance of such things as work ethic, patience, and being teachable. Oh, and respect for others!

My parents encouraged me to work during my summers while most of my friends were floating the Owens River in their inner tubes during the day and partying out in the boonies on Friday and Saturday nights. Yes, I knew my buddies were having tons of fun, but it didn't seem to matter. Before you think I missed out on anything, please realize I was spending quite a lot of time with my girlfriend. So, I wasn't really "missing out," so to speak. My priorities were just different.

But I digress. Back to entrepreneur fundamentals. My parents also taught me how to budget my money. That's how I was able to buy my first car, a 1968 Chevy Camaro, before I was even old enough to drive. Thankfully, $1,200 went a long way in 1975. Man, I wish I still had that car!

Looking back, I'm amazed at how I simply believed my parents knew more about life than any of my friends. I did what I was told (mostly), even if I didn't want to. I've thought a lot about why this was the case over the years, and the bottom line is that I simply respected my parents and didn't want to disappoint them.

Of course, they did bum me out on occasion, just as all good parents should upset their children from time to time, like when they gave me a couple of suitcases and a portable typewriter for my high school graduation. Dang. What kind of gifts are those for an eighteen-year-old? It's hard to show off brown luggage and a blue Brother typewriter. Now I know where I get my *extreme* practicality from.

TIMES HAVE CHANGED

Hopefully, you now understand why I don't have patience for people who think that simply because they have an idea and want to be an entrepreneur, somehow it is just going to magically happen. Just because you think you deserve your shot doesn't mean talent and extreme effort aren't needed—not to mention you must have an exceptional product or service people will purchase.

If you have the audacity to want to be your own boss and live life on your own terms, you had better be ready for hard work and sacrifice. If you expect to be included in the top 1 or 2 percent of wage earners in the greatest country on earth, you're going to have to be comfortable being uncomfortable.

> "Love the entrepreneur journey more than you love making money."
>
> @realKevinCortez #EmbraceTheDetour

Oh, and more than anything, you had better love the entrepreneur journey more than you love making money. Sometimes we focus so much on the destination that we forget that the journey is also part of the adventure. I believe falling in love with the journey is the ultimate gift an entrepreneur can receive.

I hope you realize that *not* being an entrepreneur can be a much better path to take in life. Actually, I've always thought being a full-time employee for a stable company with a good culture was the smart play.

Because I had considered myself more of a businessman than an entrepreneur, I wanted to have a "real" job that paid well and offered good benefits, not to mention not having to be the last line of defense when problems arose.

Call me crazy. I just thought it would be great to actually have insurance coverage and get paid time off. I also felt it would be awesome to be able to leave work at the end of the day and forget about what problems would be waiting for me back at the office.

I've never been opposed to working for a company that's *not* mine. I'm sure there are businesses out there that would give me purpose, pay well, and have wonderful coworkers I could be surrounded by.

COUNTERFEIT ENTREPRENEURS
Sometimes, the best way to define what something is is to define what it isn't. Let me try to explain what I mean through an illustration.

In the old days, before technology, one way people were trained to detect counterfeit money was to put them in a room and have everyone count real money all day long. Day after day, these individuals counted money. Why do you think they did this? How did this help with anti-counterfeiting measures?

Eventually, after several days of having the trainees count real currency, they would insert a counterfeit bill into the batches. Because the person had only been handling the real thing, they were sensitive to the look and feel of genuine bills. The moment they came into contact with the fake money, they could tell it just didn't feel right.

Please allow me a moment to dispel some of the misconceptions surrounding entrepreneurship. In this day and age of ABC's hit TV show *Shark Tank*, saying you're a *serial entrepreneur* makes you seem cool.

I've been around entrepreneurs for a few decades now. I've had the honor of personally helping several business owners address some of their greatest challenges, and I've worked closely with some incredible businesspeople who have helped me tremendously. I am *so thankful* for those relationships.

I've also suffered through working with some business owners who were just absolute tools. Can you relate? You may be surprised to learn that I'm also thankful for those negative encounters. They helped me learn what *not* to do and how *not* to act. I can now tell if someone is the "real deal" within a few moments of meeting them.

Many people with entrepreneurial tendencies would be much better off *not* launching a business just yet. Why? Because they may not have developed the stomach (or the character) for what they would actually have to go through if they were their own boss.

How do you know if you have what it takes to make it as an entrepreneur? It took me nearly thirty years to settle that question once and for all. There will always be doubts. The primary reason for writing this book was to help others answer that question for themselves.

To those of you who are in the early stages of trying to establish your business on solid footing, many challenges will press in on you, and you will definitely feel like quitting. How often? Almost every day. For those of you who are seasoned and successful entrepreneurs, I'm sure you can attest to that being true.

In 2015, I was complaining in my heart about the obstacles I had encountered in several areas of my business. As I was sitting in my chair feeling unsettled, I stepped back and carefully reexamined my situation. That's when I realized I should be over-the-moon happy. That's when I had an "aha" moment!

I was, in fact, experiencing my dream of being an entrepreneur! Despite everything pressing in all around me, I couldn't imagine living any other way. I just needed to adjust my perspective and *#EmbraceTheDetour*.

Chapter Reflections

What are your thoughts? I would love for you to share some of your answers to these questions on any of my social media platforms. Go to "KevinCortez.com" and link to them from there.

1. I reflected on how I appreciated learning the importance of a work ethic at a young age. Can you identify a time in your life when you realized the value of work in your character development?

2. You're reading this book for a reason: an experience or event has prompted you to explore more information on entrepreneurship. How do you define an *entrepreneur*?

3. What went through your mind when I said, "You had better love the entrepreneur journey more than you love making money?"

Scan the QR code for bonus content.

CHAPTER 3

The Dream of an Entrepreneur

W hen I was getting ready to graduate from junior college in 1980, I wanted to attend California Polytechnic. The problem was that I had my heart set on majoring in Business Administration but didn't have the grades to be accepted into that program. I picked a major that was close but had a lot less math: Recreation Administration.

My dream was to one day own a health club, so I figured studying the recreation industry, along with taking as many business classes as possible using my electives, would provide the necessary skill set to run a business in that industry. At least, that was my reasoning.

By the time I entered my senior year at Cal Poly, I had accumulated enough electives in the Business Administration curriculum to take various senior-level courses in that major. One of those courses became the best class I ever took.

The professor divided the class into small teams and tasked each team with creating a business plan. At the end of the semester, each team would go before real investors and pitch their start-up business idea. Kinda like the Emmy-winning ABC reality show *Shark Tank*, right?

Since I was the only non-business major in the class, I could tell that no one wanted me on their team. I felt like that kid on the playground who would always get picked last to be on someone's dodgeball team. Do they even allow kids to play dodgeball these days? I did break my arm playing that wild game in elementary school, so I guess it can be dangerous.

I thought my fellow students were correct in their assumptions since they were "real" business majors, and I was the guy getting a degree in *Leisure Engineering*. They grudgingly assigned me to work on the marketing portion of the business plan since I was then the university's College Marketing Representative for the Coors Brewing Company. Really. That was my actual job (which made me very popular with the fraternities on campus).

Then a funny thing happened as I met with the other students. Almost immediately, my team members appeared clueless when it came to having to apply what they'd been taught the previous four years to a real-life business concept. We came up with a good idea, but they started to freak out over the fact that the entire grade in the class rested on how our idea was going to be judged by real business investors and not the professor.

For whatever reason, I ended up being the only one in the group who could pull together what had been assigned. After three group meetings, they made me team leader. I found that ironic.

What they hadn't known was that I'd been working on a type of business plan for my Senior Project, a capstone experience required for all Cal Poly students receiving a baccalaureate degree. The Senior Project typically takes one-and-a-half years to complete, and it is designed to integrate theory and application from across the student's undergraduate educational experiences.

My Senior Project was based on the feasibility of opening a health club in my hometown of Bishop. I had to take into account all the variables of starting a real business in a particular city during a specific year. That project became my first full-blown business plan. That was also the first time I realized that just because you have a good idea for a business, it doesn't mean the business will be successful.

I discovered Bishop could not support a health club in any form in 1983. Going into the project, I really thought it could. But when all the information I had gathered was analyzed, I was wrong. I had made the mistake many entrepreneurs make: I had romanticized the idea.

And in case you're wondering, yes, the business plan my team presented to the investors in that class was well-received. I'd like to think we got an A for our plan mainly because of the guy no one wanted on their team. Ta-da!

From that experience, I realized that just because you have a college degree in a specific field doesn't mean it will automatically translate into real-world success. This is especially true in entrepreneurship.

HIGHER EDUCATION UPDATE

I've worked with several MBA interns from one of the top programs in the country. They all had big entrepreneurial dreams and were quick to identify themselves as *serial entrepreneurs*. They had no idea how ill-equipped they were for the real world of business ownership. But they were perfectly educated for jobs that no longer exist.

A few things: first, just like with everything, there are exceptions. I'm sure some MBA students end up making it big as entrepreneurs. Second, the students I worked with were paying over $119,000 for a graduate degree, and that didn't even include how much money they had spent on their undergrad education and living expenses. Lastly, they were great kids, but from my perspective, all they seemed to be learning in their classes was outdated theoretical tactics. But they did know a lot of fancy business buzzwords I'd never heard before.

When I would talk to some of their professors, I was amazed at how completely caught-up Dr. Disconnected was in *how it used to be*. It was downright scary how these educators didn't realize they were several years behind what was actually transpiring in today's business environment. It was even more terrifying to think about what those students would emotionally endure after graduation.

In my humble opinion, our educational model is outdated and not designed to keep pace with the challenges and opportunities of the rapid shifts in the market. Business schools are sending out Fred Flintstones into a George Jetson world. What these schools are teaching is far from practical.

Don't misunderstand me. I am not throwing shade on the education system. Well, maybe a little. OK, I guess I'm being super critical. Some students may learn how to contribute to a big corporation, but there is simply no traditional school on earth that exists which can remotely educate a student properly on entrepreneurship and marketing in the world in which we live.

Hear what I'm saying, and don't hear what I'm not saying: Don't think I'm telling someone *not* to go to college. Look, if you have the money and desire to pay for a degree, I get it. There are positive life experiences a student can have … and connections they can make in a college setting that might benefit their future.

I am so grateful for the opportunity I had to attend a prominent university when I did, back when a college degree was one of the few benchmarks that created opportunity. Yes, I took away some things that I appreciate, but I believe the most valuable lesson I gained from college was *learning how to learn*. And nowadays, the Internet search engine Google offers that for free.

This has translated extremely well in my chosen field. If I need to know something, I can learn it online. And since I want to learn everything I can about marketing and emerging media, I spend countless hours online consuming relevant content from people who have legitimate businesses and are actually doing the work.

Here's the punch line: if you want to attend college, that's great—as long as you don't collect any debt in doing so. Debt drags you down. In case you've missed what I'm advocating, here it is again: ***don't go into debt to attend college!***

I remember when Ernst & Young, one of the top graduate recruiters in the world, dropped the bombshell a couple of years ago that they would no longer require college degrees for job candidates applying to join their teams. They said, "[We] found no evidence to conclude that previous success in higher education correlated with future success in subsequent professional qualifications undertaken."[4] This was a big deal when it was announced. Now, since the list of major employers that no longer require a college degree has grown exponentially, it doesn't even make the news.

Disclaimer: I know you need to have a college degree to be a doctor or engineer. But this book is about entrepreneurship and not about becoming an architect or lawyer. I just believe we need to stop promoting higher education at the expense of every other form of learning. I simply reject the popular notion that a four-year degree is the best path for the most people. And I'm hardly alone.

I think about it this way: colleges are actually first and foremost businesses, and they are structured to make money just like every other business. Period. Also, like other businesses, they offer a product (knowledge) to consumers (students). Unfortunately, colleges continue to raise prices on their failing product. Can anyone explain to me why a textbook costs over $200?

So, the question becomes: "Why would anyone in their right mind buy such an expensive product that is basically worthless?"

I can answer that: because colleges have done a tremendous job branding themselves as being necessary if you want to have a successful career and get ahead in life.

For the life of me, I can't understand why someone who's supposed to be so smart takes out a loan (with compound interest) that they will be paying on for several years after they leave college—which, by the way, they can't get out of through declaring bankruptcy. Now, factor in how those monthly student loan payments take away so many options when you're trying to gain momentum after graduation. This terrible debt structure can really set a person back. Frankly, that's just messed up. Feel free to disagree.

Actually, the only people I could see arguing with my logic are those in the education system (and benefitting from it). Or, maybe those individuals who have an emotional attachment to the idea that higher learning has somehow made them more intelligent than those who haven't had the opportunity to attend college. They may take issue with my thesis. I bump into that smug, condescending attitude every so often.

Oh, I almost forgot to mention: those parents who have their self-esteem tied to whether or not their children attend college. That should be part of this conversation. Mom and/or Dad may disagree with my observations because they think their kid's accomplishments reflect their parenting, so ... there's that. But just ask any small business owner what their take is on this subject and see what they say.

If you're thinking, "But Kevin, I've already accumulated that debt you're talking about. What do I do now?" I respect that financial debt is a real hardship. Thankfully, you're living at a time unlike any other in history. With your smartphone, laptop, and an Internet connection, you can still win. My experiences have taught me that anything, *anything* is possible.

"With a smartphone, laptop, and Internet connection, you can win."

@realKevinCortez #EmbraceTheDetour

The market doesn't care about how much debt you do or don't have. For the record, the market also doesn't care about your skin color, age, gender, zip code, connections, or education. The unique opportunity to succeed as an entrepreneur is available to everyone, regardless of what you may have been told.

THE DREAM
You may be reading this and have the same entrepreneurial dream I had when I was working with those students back at Cal Poly: one day, I want to run my own business. If so, that's fantastic.

Why do you have that dream? The reasons for having an entrepreneurial dream are as unique as the persons having them.

Many people think living the entrepreneurial dream is all about making more money, working fewer hours, and being able to do what they love. This is constantly reinforced by individuals claiming that they've done it and promising that, if you do what they tell you to do, you can be just like them and have the financial means to do whatever you want, whenever you want.

Others think being an entrepreneur means having the freedom to be your own boss and never having to be at the mercy of someone else.

Does any of this make you happy? Maybe yes, maybe no. If yes, for how long? What you may not have been told is that you're going to spend over 90 percent of your time every working day doing boring things that aren't even remotely fun—especially in the beginning stages of your business. But those of you who are already entrepreneurs know this to be true, and I'm guessing you still wouldn't want to have it any other way.

For me, the reason I wanted to be an entrepreneur started out simply: there was just something in me that thought owning my own business was what I was meant to do. It wasn't any more complicated than that.

"The number one dream assassin is impatience."

@realKevinCortez #EmbraceTheDetour

What I hadn't prepared for was how long it would actually take to realize that dream. I knew there were several things that could kill my dream—people, lack of resources, timing, distractions, etc.—but the number one "dream assassin" I encountered was impatience. Some things you just can't rush, and entrepreneurship is one of those things.

A WARNING

I am fascinated by individuals who have *never* built a business outside of creating a company that "teaches" you how to build a business. Selling stuff to those wanting to succeed at being an entrepreneur has become a lucrative business for some. The dream of owning your own business powerfully affects one's emotions.

There are a lot of "experts" who know how to tap into entrepreneurs' emotions and convince them that what they're selling will help the entrepreneur realize their dream. In their carnival-barker-meets-used-car-salesman presentations, much of it is smoke and mirrors, and they are taking advantage of people while lining their pockets.

Believe me. I know what I'm talking about. "How?" you say. Well, I've thrown thousands of dollars at some of the top small business "experts" and online marketing "gurus" myself.

At first, I naively thought they actually wanted to help my entrepreneurial dream become a reality. I've traveled to several cities across this great land and have sat in their multiple-day events listening to their wisdom from on high.

Much of what they said was somewhat relevant but certainly not profound. Because I'd already built a few successful businesses, I could recognize when what they were espousing was outdated or, in many cases, completely wrong. In fact, it was so wrong that if you were to take their advice, it would end up setting your business back. In some cases, permanently.

It didn't take too long before I began to see a pattern emerge with some of these knuckleheads. The ones I'm referring to all seem to have one theme in common: everything they talked about was always followed by a sales pitch. And, of course, their various presentations would have the standard "scarcity" and "sense of urgency" built into them.

Naturally, the *sage from the stage* would never forget to include an "upsell" for those who took the bait—I mean, purchased their offer. The upsell encouraged them to part with even more of their dollars. In fact, if you wanted, you could even learn how to "sell from the stage" just like them—for $20,000. Oh, puh-leeze. Give me a break.

Even knowing this, I am still willing to set aside my time and give some of them my attention. I try to believe the best in someone until they show me otherwise. Thankfully I'm able to figure out what is real and what isn't before losing too much of my hard-earned money on their special, today-only, exclusive offers.

Unfortunately, it bugs me when I watch aspiring entrepreneurs turn over thousands of dollars (that they don't have) to some clown-biscuit who is blatantly taking advantage of the fact that they have a dream of becoming a more successful business owner. Can you tell this really winds me up? This anger is one of the primary motivators that helped me set aside the time needed to create this book.

I totally understand the lure. Seeing someone fly around in a private jet and talk about having millionaires and billionaires in their contact list is impressive. But it doesn't mean they actually care about helping you with your entrepreneurial dream. Don't be sucked in by the photos on their marketing materials of themselves posing with famous people. After all, this is the era of the "selfie."

Beware of those who are always showing off their "stuff." All of this does not necessarily equate to them knowing how to help you grow your specific business. Did you know that some of those houses, cars, and watches in their videos aren't really theirs? You can rent or borrow anything these days.

I'm no expert, and I can't prove it, but if I had to guess, I believe you'll be able to see these pitchmen and hucksters coming from a mile away after you read this book. That alone could be worth thousands of dollars to you. So, make sure you read this entire book at least once.

How's that for a shameless sales pitch?

GO FOR IT

What is your entrepreneurial dream? There has never been a better time than now to become bold in pursuing that dream. I believe the future belongs to successful entrepreneurs. If you have the desire, I say *GO FOR IT*!

If there is an entrepreneur in you dying to be let out, allow it to step out. Overcome your self-doubt and see if you have what it takes. If realizing your entrepreneurial dream never happens, you will still be a better person for having tried. You don't want to look back at this time in your life and regret not trying.

When you go after a big dream, you will always hear from those who think small. Who cares what the naysayers say? When you dare to take that step, you will be surrounded by those who'd rather you stay put. Small-minded people will always try to talk you out of your dreams.

You're holding this book in your hands because you are (or want to be) an entrepreneur. I hope what I share about my journey helps you and strengthens your resolve to be one of those heroes I look up to.

If some of what you read seems like I'm trying to talk you out of becoming an entrepreneur, you're correct. Entrepreneurship isn't for everyone.

I figure if you know what gut-wrenching experiences actually happen to all entrepreneurs and that doesn't scare you away, then you're ready to face what is sure to be a steady stream of challenges. If you've counted the cost and know you have the stomach for it, then you're ready to *#EmbraceTheDetour*.

Chapter Reflections

What are your thoughts? I would love for you to share some of your answers to these questions on any of my social media platforms. Go to "KevinCortez.com" and link to them from there.

1. Do you have an entrepreneurship dream? Are you on the road to realizing that dream? If yes, awesome. If not, why not?

2. Were you encouraged or offended when you read that I believe college can't prepare you for entrepreneurship? Do you have firsthand knowledge of this topic?

3. Do you understand why I get so upset over those who rip off entrepreneurs? Have you ever been taken advantage of by one of those clown-biscuits I refer to?

Scan the QR Code for bonus content.

CHAPTER 4

The Perspective
of an Entrepreneur

As I entered into my early thirties, I had the most incredible job. The organization I'd been working for since moving to Dallas had grown exponentially, and I'd grown with it. When I took that $4.50-per-hour job delivering TV and radio programs to local broadcast stations, the International Christian Ministry and Outreach Center had approximately three hundred employees. Eight years later, we were one of the top three largest organizations of our type in the world, employing over two thousand people.

When a business experiences that kind of growth, it creates all kinds of opportunities for its employees (if they are capable and trustworthy). I learned so many job skills in the different areas I served. And with each new promotion, I developed unique attributes to deal with the more significant challenges.

I was very fortunate to be given opportunities I wasn't ready for right out of college. I worked hard and learned that if I didn't have an answer, I'd ask a lot of questions and figure it out.

When I think about the time I had twenty-one direct reports and managed over 250 employees when I was in my twenties, it still freaks me out a little. Now that was a challenge.

But the last position I held, Special Projects Coordinator, was by far the most enjoyable. I felt like everything I'd ever learned at every job I'd ever had came into play. Whatever "special project" our visionary CEO and leader thought up (that was "outside the ordinary"), it was my job to figure out how to garner the resources and make it happen. When someone would ask what my job entailed, I'd say *I help build rocket ships as they're taking off from the launching pad.* It was the typical "Fire–Ready–Aim" stuff.

As much as I loved my job, my entrepreneurial desires began to surface more frequently as the years unfolded. Whenever I thought about my future, that dream of running my own business was still a part of who I was deep down in my heart and soul.

Since I was the oldest of three children in my family and seemingly the only one interested in the business, I'd always felt that one day I would be the one to take over the beer distributorship from my father. But I just wasn't sure if moving back to California and working for Eastern Sierra Wholesalers would be the right move for me.

Still, I went ahead and called my dad and told him that if a position became available at the company, I'd like to be considered—if it made sense.

TIME FOR A CHANGE

After Prohibition ended in 1933, the US government divided the beer industry into three tiers: manufacturers, wholesalers, and retailers. The middlemen in this arrangement are the independent wholesale beer distributors. Breweries produce the beer, distributors transport and sell it to retailers, and retailers sell the beer to the public.

In the world of regulated alcohol distribution, most distributorships have been family-owned for generations. Typical owners had grown up working in the business since childhood. Since I didn't work in the family business in my youth, I was the exception.

When I was in my late teens, I had a conversation with my dad about this. He thought it would be better for me if I did *not* work at Eastern Sierra Wholesalers so I could learn how to succeed without relying on a "safety net" that may or may not be there in the future. His reasoning seemed sound: if something were ever to happen and the company wasn't there to support me, I could still "make it out in the real world" because I'd learned how.

I figured since my dad had had a career before going to work at Eastern Sierra, he had a good perspective on the whole thing. It turns out he was more right than anyone knew, especially in my case.

Incidentally, I've shared this same advice with several family-run business owners, but, for whatever reason, they nodded their heads though I could tell that my advice was going in one ear and out the other. Most believed they were helping their kids by getting them involved in the family business as early as possible. Who am I to judge? Maybe that was the best thing in their children's cases— or perhaps it wasn't. I've already seen it play out negatively in several instances. Time always has a way of revealing the right choice in those scenarios.

MAKING INFORMED DECISIONS

My dad called me a few months after our initial conversation to tell me that his sales manager had taken another job and would be leaving soon. He thought it might be a good idea for me to spend a week with the manager before he left to see if his job was something I'd be interested in doing. Since I felt like I'd "made it" in Dallas, I figured it might be an excellent time to explore putting myself into a position of taking my shot at being an entrepreneur.

Some of you reading this may think having an opportunity like that was a no-brainer, but that wasn't the case. There was much to consider: not only would I be taking a substantial pay cut while moving to a place where the standard of living was much higher, but I would also be going into an increasingly volatile industry.

Beer distribution has seen significant changes over the last few decades. Through consolidations, the number of traditional beer distributors has fallen over 35 percent.[5] That means over sixteen hundred families are no longer owners of beverage distributorships in one generation. And those consolidations continue to this day.[6] I often wonder how some of those owners who were raised in the business and knew nothing else are doing in this economy.

I flew out to California and spent a week in the business. I brought back five years of income statements and balance sheets. I wanted to know exactly what I'd be walking into. First, I compared Eastern Sierra's health to the *1990 Annual Statement Studies* by Robert Morris Associates and *Industry Norms and Key Business Ratios* by Dun and Bradstreet.

In case you're wondering, financial ratios are often used to compare a company against an industry average (or other companies) to benchmark a company's performance and potential. Since the resource books I used were extremely expensive, I went to one of the university libraries in Dallas and made copies of the pages I needed. For those of you who are business nerds, I used *SIC Code 5181 (82)* for *Wholesalers – Wine, Liquor, and Beer (NAICS 424810)*.

Industry ratios are often useful when creating the financial components of a business plan. I spent the next few months researching the latest industry trends to see what direction it was moving … and to also see how Eastern Sierra Wholesalers stacked up against comparable distributorships. Man, I sure was glad I'd done that type of research a few times before.

I put together a detailed company profile for myself, which revealed that the business was in a solid financial position. This was great news, but when I factored in the industry trends, the data indicated we had about five years before the company would go the way of several of the other distributorships if something didn't dramatically change.

Now, if a typical commonsense business analyst were to go over what I'd put together, they would have advised me to "stay far away from that company." But the perspective of an entrepreneur is usually very different from bean-counter types. Entrepreneurs know that the entire story of a company cannot be determined by reading the black-and-white columns of a profit-and-loss statement. When I showed my father what I'd put together, he seemed unfazed. Dismissive even. In his mind, well, I didn't know what he was thinking.

THE ENTREPRENEUR PERSPECTIVE

I tried to grasp what it would look like going into the family business in the next few months. I rolled several of the variables around in my head: the people I'd be working with, moving back to the small town I'd grown up in, selling products I had absolutely no interest in (I don't even drink), taking a significant pay cut, and the volatile nature of the beverage industry—not to mention the complex layers of working alongside family members.

There were just so many constraints when I looked at what was before me. So, I did what any other entrepreneur would do: as I studied the information I had put together, I figured out how to best prepare myself for the fight ahead. Here's some profound advice: don't take on entrepreneurship unless you are ready for a battle. Entrepreneurship is a contact sport. If you can't stand the sight of your own blood, don't become an entrepreneur.

Part of handling the stress of being an entrepreneur is being able to choose one thought over another. You must have the mindset that says, "I'm fighting for a future and the life of my business," because you just might be. Entrepreneurs with self-confidence know that no matter the challenge, they'll pull it off and succeed. This is the only perspective to have in order to engage in the battle correctly. If you have any other perspective, you will quit when the going gets tough. And if you don't know already, it will get tough.

> ## "Don't take on entrepreneurship unless you are ready for a battle."
>
> @realKevinCortez #EmbraceTheDetour

You may have guessed it by now. Yes. I moved back to my hometown to work for the company my grandfather began forty-five years earlier. Goodbye, "fastest-growing ministry in America." Hello, beer, wine, and liquor distributorship out in the middle of nowhere.

Some of my close friends who knew the details of what I was about to do thought I was crazy. They believed I had one of the best gigs going in Dallas. Other buddies considered the chance at eventually running a corporation annually generating multi-million-dollar revenue was my best move.

How you see yourself in a particular situation will determine how you proceed. Entrepreneurs see the potential in everything and everyone. I'd already thought through various worst-case scenarios, but I was confident that whatever was thrown at me, I would rise to the occasion.

My decision to move proved to be the right one almost immediately. Guess what happened two weeks after I arrived in California? The organization I had just left began to implode. Its charismatic leader had made some wrong choices which set in motion my former employer's downfall. And great was its fall!

My heart broke as I watched from fifteen hundred miles away as those unwise actions led to the entire organization eventually closing its doors. This negatively affected so many people, including several of my dear friends. Argh!

BUSINESS IS THE ULTIMATE SPORT

Just like entrepreneurship, sports can be cruel—at least for the loser. And if you were to ask me, tennis can be the cruelest of them all. Seriously, I could make an excellent case for tennis being one of the most challenging sports. Let the debate begin…

Tennis is a gladiator-esque event that leaves the loser heartbroken and physically spent, and it can mess with your mind in so many different ways. Think about it. You don't have your teammates, caddy, or support staff to help you while you're competing. And at its inevitable conclusion, there can be only one winner, who is right there across the net celebrating and adding insult to injury. It is, in fact, a cruel, cruel sport.

I was eighteen when I touched my first tennis racquet. I asked my friend Wayne's older sister, who I knew played tennis, to give me a lesson before I went off to Cuesta Junior College in San Luis Obispo. I'd signed up for Intermediate Tennis and figured since I was a decent athlete, if she just taught me how to hold the racquet for the different shots and how to keep score, I could skip the beginner classes altogether. I know. I was being extremely presumptuous—it went with being eighteen.

Right when I arrived in San Luis, I found a tennis court with a "hitting wall" and practiced my shots against that wall for a couple of hours. I didn't want to be too embarrassed before my first class the next day. During that first class, our instructor, Ms. Frey, asked if I had played any competitive tennis before. (I thought she was teasing me.) I just laughed and said it was only my third time playing. She asked if I would practice some specific things after each class, and I said, "Sure." A few weeks later, Ms. Frey moved me into her advanced class.

When I start something, I typically go all in. Once I lock on, I tend to be rather obsessive. Add my competitiveness to that, and things can become very intense (just ask anyone in my family).

I wasn't expecting to do anything with tennis but just make some friends and have fun. Then, once I started, I got addicted. I absolutely loved the sport because whatever happened, win or lose, it was up to me (like entrepreneurship can be). I ended up playing or practicing three to five hours a day. I just couldn't get enough.

After a few months, I was the top player in the advanced class, and Ms. Frey thought I should try out for the college's tennis team. I did and ended up making it onto the varsity squad, which played the other junior colleges in our conference. The two years I was on the team were awesome. We even went undefeated. Go Cuesta Cougars!

For my last collegiate match, I made it to the quarterfinals of the Central California Community College Championships. I was playing the number one player from another school, and it looked like I was about to win until the momentum shifted. Even though the opponent was behind and about to lose, he finally figured out my biggest weakness: just make me hit a high backhand. Once he saw how to deal with my serve-and-volley and get me to hit a backhand, he came roaring back in the match and ended my intercollegiate athletic career that day.

I still had big tennis dreams until I watched some fourteen-year-old girl play in a tournament I was playing in a few weeks later. Reality check. I knew that young girl would smoke me. Oh well. Goodbye, tennis dream. That's why I think tennis is a cruel sport.

<u>Side Note</u>: now I had to find a new activity. Ever since my dad had taken me to my first R-rated movie, *Enter the Dragon,* starring Bruce Lee, when I was thirteen years old, I wanted to learn martial arts. So that's what I threw myself into next.

How does this relate to me going into the family business? I wanted you to have a little more understanding of what my personality is like. I took that same passion, dedication, focus, and any natural talent I had available and directed it toward growing our family's beverage distributorship.

I knew that since I happened to have the owner's last name, I would have to work harder than the other employees. I didn't show up at the business and kick back, not worrying about anything because I had job security. I had a big chip on my shoulder (in a good way). Since I never wanted my name and "nepotism" to be used in the same sentence, I was constantly trying to work to the best of my abilities.

Business is the ultimate sport. Your competition, along with all the other market forces, is always trying to "take you out." Fortunately, it's like tennis, where it's not over until the last point is played. As long as you're still on the tennis court, the game isn't over.

Even though your opponent has a match point, there's still a chance to defy all odds and win. Just don't be surprised if it takes longer than expected to win, like the crazy match held during the 2010 Wimbledon Tennis Championships that required eleven hours and five minutes (stretching to three days) for the American John Isner to beat the Frenchman Nicolas Mahut.

Since I was hired as the Sales Manager at Eastern Sierra Wholesalers, I aggressively looked for ways to increase sales. I wanted to absolutely crush my competitors. The beverage market was shifting, our sales had been stagnant, profit margins had been progressively decreasing for years, we were losing entire product lines due to consolidations, and I just knew something out of the box needed to be done.

REACTING TO THE MARKET

My first bold move was to diversify what products we sold. We had trucks making deliveries to all the grocery stores, restaurants, convenience stores, and any other retail outlets that sold alcohol in our area. I figured it made sense to have those trucks deliver as many products as possible, and I didn't care what type of beverages they were.

A few months after moving back, I was talking to my friend Matt on the phone. I told him what I was up to, and he asked me if I had ever heard of a flavored iced tea called Snapple. I hadn't. He said he'd tried a bottle in the San Diego area and loved its taste.

I called around, did some research, and finally found the person responsible for Snapple's distribution. I told her about our beer distributorship and asked if we could be Snapple's exclusive distributor for our area. They sent someone to interview me and look over our operations. We ended up with an agreement, and I was super pumped to see that big semitruck pulling into our docks with our first shipment a few weeks later.

But then I overheard some rumblings among the Easter Sierra Wholesalers crew:

"What's Snapple?"

"We're beer guys. We don't sell fruity teas."

"What does Kevin think he's doing?"

"No one is going to buy that #$@&%*! Those same pallets we just unloaded are going to be sitting in the warehouse a year from now."

Fortunately, our sales team did an excellent job executing the rollout. The following week we had to bring in two more shipments. Within a few short months, sales had taken off. Before all was said and done, we had the highest "bottle-per-capita ratio" in the country (units sold compared to the population). We also added customers who didn't have the licensing to sell alcohol. Did I mention that the profit margin of those fruity teas was three times better than any beer we sold? It was a beautiful thing!

I believe that one decision was critical to the survival of our distributorship. Not too long after bringing in Snapple, we lost our entire liquor line of products. Eastern Sierra was one of the 116 liquor distributors in the state that lost those product lines through consolidations. California was now left with only two liquor distributors.

The Snapple victory motivated me more than ever to keep diversifying. Next, I secured the distribution rights of a little 8.4-ounce can of awful-tasting stuff I heard was popular with the snowboarders over in Europe. Again, more rumblings ensued:

"No one in their right mind would spend over two dollars for a tiny can of something that doesn't have any alcohol in it."

"What kind of name is Red Bull?

"Who ever heard of drinking something specifically designed to give you a burst of energy?"

Well, that little expensive can of awful-tasting stuff with a weird name made our company *a lot* of money!

I was on a roll. Soon we were distributing snacks and bar supplies. If you wanted glassware, napkins, TVs, olives, or whatever else your bar needed, we could get it for you. Eventually, the employees stopped criticizing what I was doing (at least that I knew of).

Ohmigosh, I was having a blast and giving our competitors fits. They really had to step up their game big-time to keep up with what we were doing.

It wasn't too long before my dad promoted me to General Manager. I then turned my attention to the operations side of the business. Now it was time for our office employees to stretch a little bit.

Some of the admin personnel were *not* too happy with me as I automated and systematized everything using state-of-the-art technology. But transforming the distributorship to run like a much bigger player in the game put us in the position to have the largest wine and liquor distributor in the country turn their entire portfolio over to us. That's another fun story for another time. Let me reiterate: "Luck is when opportunity meets preparation."

After a couple of years at Eastern Sierra, my dad felt comfortable with me running everything, so he decided to retire. Now it was all on me. Kinda. It wasn't as daunting as it sounds because I knew my father was always there if I needed his help in any way.

What I remember most about that period of my life was the incredible support I received from our various suppliers: Coors, Snapple, Quaker Oats, Red Bull, and other manufacturers. They would help us with business plans, marketing campaigns, sales planning, operations, budgeting, and anything else we needed to be a successful business.

I'd ask myself on several occasions, "How in the world do small-business owners make it without this kind of support?"

The market is constantly tearing you down. The problems an entrepreneur faces are relentless, and there are no time-outs. Every day, we battle something that's trying to pull our businesses apart.

Different people have different battles, but everybody has something they are struggling to overcome. Simply recognizing this fact sometimes makes the struggle a little easier.

I had the amazing fortune of being able to pick up the phone and ask for a consultation from individuals who really knew their stuff.

REBOOT

After about thirteen years at Eastern Sierra, I felt like I had flatlined. Even though our industry was in turmoil, our revenue had tripled since I'd started working there. But we'd hit a ceiling. Sales had plateaued. It just wasn't fun or challenging anymore. I felt constrained. If I were to sum up the biggest problem in one word, that word is *California.*

According to the *Annual Chief Executive.net Survey*, at that time, California was the absolute worst state to do business in.[7] While writing this chapter in 2017, I looked up the Golden State's current ranking out of curiosity. It had successfully defended its "worst state" crown—for the twelfth straight year in a row.

Can you spell D-E-N-I-A-L?

This annual survey of 500 CEOs from across America highlights California's state and local government officials' negative attitudes toward business. CEOs blamed the cost of trying to comply with the state's arbitrary, irrational, or outdated regulatory system.

Over the years, survey after survey has shown California is an awful place to do business in, especially for smaller companies that are the least able to bear the costs. The top officials and politicians believe it's all rainbows, butterflies, and unicorns, but I can attest that the surveys are legit. In my experience, those running the state really are the latter half of *Dumb & Dumber*.

Our family business had been stifled and smothered with one unnecessary hindrance after another. The burdens of being overtaxed and overregulated sucked the life out of me. Our company was stable, but I could tell it was time for me to make some changes. So I did. I turned the business over to the capable hands of my younger brother, Jon. Thankfully, once again, my parents were very supportive.

Guess what state the Chief Executive Survey indicated was the best place to do business year-after-year? Yep. The Lone Star State of Texas. Yippie-ki-yay!

Here we go again.

Did I find it difficult to step away from something I had envisioned for my life since a young age? You bet I did! Especially considering I only had about three months of finances to live on—six months if I cashed out my life insurance policy (which I ended up having to do).

Reset. I decided to risk it all, move back to Dallas, and *#EmbraceTheDetour*.

Chapter Reflections

What are your thoughts? I would love for you to share some of your answers to these questions on any of my social media platforms. Go to "KevinCortez.com" and link to them from there.

1. When I shared my thought process before making a decision to move halfway across the country and completely change the direction of my life, could you relate? Have you ever wanted to do something radical like that?

2. What did you think of my advice *not* to take on entrepreneurship unless you are ready for a battle? Are you ready?

3. In light of business being the ultimate sport, what steps can you take today to be more competitive with your business?

Scan the QR Code for bonus content.

CHAPTER 5

The Choices
of an Entrepreneur

When the plane touched down in the middle of the night at O'Hare International Airport in Chicago, I had a glimpse of what was in store for the next few weeks. Stepping out of the terminal, I saw a guy standing on the curb next to a white limousine holding a sign with the name *Kevin Cortez*.

"Hey, that's me."

As I got into the car and looked at the minibar, I thought, *These guys are serious.*

As the limo driver dropped me off forty-five minutes later at an upscale hotel, he told me a shuttle would pick me up in the morning at 7:40 a.m. The following day, nineteen other "recruits" and I gathered in the hotel lobby. A shuttle rolled up at 7:40 a.m. sharp to take us to the training facilities. Let the games begin.

It was May 2006. I had just gone through a two-month hiring cycle with this leading privately held management consulting firm. It had started with over a thousand applicants being considered for a Senior Business Consultant position. Eventually, after three phone interviews, I was one of approximately a hundred candidates who'd made it to the in-person interview.

Mr. Fancy Suit, from the Recruiting Department, flew to Dallas for my interview. After only three questions, he invited me to their headquarters for training.

I said, "That's it?"

He said, "I can typically figure out within sixty seconds if someone has a chance of making it through our training program."

Wait. What the what?

I had no idea what "make it" meant.

I decided to keep my mouth shut, simply thank him for the opportunity, and get out of there before he changed his mind.

GAME ON

As we pulled up to the training building, I had no idea what to expect from this company that was generating revenues of more than $250 million and had over two thousand employees. Imagine sitting in a room with twenty highly experienced, take-charge, outgoing professionals who each had at least ten-plus years of senior-level management experience and/or business ownership. Now, imagine that at the end of each training day, you were ranked from one to twenty based on how you measured up against the others; one was the best, and twenty was, well, not the best.

Most of that first day was everyone "selling themselves" to our two trainers, Richard and Dawn. I thought I would have had some sort of advantage in making an impression since I had recently finished training to be an Executive Business Analyst for their main competitor. At the competitor's firm, I had been trained to perform comprehensive examinations on the financial, operational, and sales functions of small- to medium-sized businesses—so I naturally threw out every consulting industry buzzword I knew.

At the end of the opening day of training, the number given to me was twenty. Well, I guess the only way I can go now is up. By the third day, I had climbed to fourteen in this pack of overachievers. I couldn't get too excited because six individuals had already been "invited to leave," and none of us knew why.

Over the course of the next couple of weeks, this organization threw some very intense training at us. When the dust finally settled, there were only five of us left. Where did I end up in the class ranking? I'm glad you asked: I received the top honors in my training class. Number one sounds better than number twenty, don't you think?

I was so grateful to have learned some impressive aspects of running a business. I was also shocked to learn just how little I actually knew about some critical areas of being an entrepreneur. But what I was really happy about was that I was finally in a position to bring some help to struggling business owners.

I remember being so thankful for the support I had received when I was running our family business, and now I could be the one providing practical management support to entrepreneurs.

GETTING PAID TO LEARN

Over the next year, I traveled throughout the United States and Canada helping small business owners address some of their greatest challenges. I was typically on the road from Sunday afternoon through Friday evening every single week. Ugh! The travel was brutal. But since I really wanted to learn the consultancy business model, I just looked at it as though I was getting paid to learn how to implement a consultancy project. Plus, I was racking up some serious air miles and hotel points.

The way our consultancy projects worked was: first, our firm's sales team would contact a business owner to see if they would like to have their business evaluated. If they did, an analyst would fly to the business's location and spend a couple of days performing an exhaustive diagnostic assessment.

Next, if it was determined that there was an opportunity to bring in a consultant to resolve the issues identified during the analysis, a Project Manager and a Senior Business Consultant (me) would arrive the next day.

Then, after a day and a half of getting to know the business on a deeper level, the Project Manager put together a plan of action if things looked like they could move forward. Lastly, the Project Manager left, and I would stay behind to start working on the plan with the owner and key decision makers.

Our consulting engagements could last from a few weeks to a few months. If the business owner didn't like how the "Value Enhancement Program" was progressing, they could suspend the project at the end of any day. Since my firm was charging $325 an hour, plus expenses for me

to "do my thing," the pressure was on for me to show *a
lot* of value every day!

I am proud to say that the only times I did not complete
the entire scope of work was when the business's budget
did not allow the project plan to continue.

Can I tell you a big secret? On some of the projects, I
was the one who suspended the engagement. I believed
that having the business spend $12,000 to $14,000 each
week for my services was not in the business owner's best
interest.

I knew I was taking the risk of being benched from the
good projects if a Project Manager (or my employer)
found out that I was the one who had put the brakes on
everything. But I felt it was more important to do the right
thing for the owner than for me to stay just so my firm
could have more billable hours from me.

After spending an amazing year learning how to better
serve small to midsize businesses and acquiring some
incredible skills, I started my own consulting agency
called Entrust Management Solutions.

I modified several tactics in how I helped my clients
make distinctive, lasting, and substantial improvements in
their businesses.

For example, instead of me executing all of the
necessary changes in a matter of weeks, I put together a
practical plan the business could implement themselves
over the course of a year (with my help).

I would spend ten to twenty hours a month giving them
hands-on support and strategic direction. And did I
mention my rates were not nearly as expensive as they
were previously? What a deal.

KNOW YOUR VITAL SIGNS

As an entrepreneur, staying on course can be overwhelming: there is often too much to do in too little time with too little money.

According to those who know about such things, over 90 percent of businesses fail before their ten-year anniversary. Seven out of ten new companies will likely survive for only two years, and half of the startups will only stay open for five years. Those staggering statistics make me mad! Why? Because a lot of those failures didn't have to happen.

Why do most businesses fail? Because they can't pay their bills. Duh! When you run out of cash, it's game over. Your most important financial decisions should not be about how to make money but how to keep it, grow it, and maximize it.

> "Your most important financial decisions should not be about how to make money but how to keep it, grow it, and maximize it."
>
> @realKevinCortez #EmbraceTheDetour

Think of a business you know of that looked like it was doing fine on the surface, but, one day they just closed their doors. The business had customers, sold a great product, the service was pretty good, and the owner was working really, really hard, but the business is now gone. What happened?

From what I've observed from working in the trenches with hundreds of businesses, the owner running the business probably didn't even know they had a serious problem until it was too late. They had no idea what was silently sabotaging their financial results. And the primary reason they didn't know was that they didn't bother to gain an understanding of how to look at their financial indicators. If you were to ask them, they would most likely tell you they didn't even look at their financials. And if they did, they would admit to you they didn't have a clue as to what their financials really meant.

Many entrepreneurs just look at the bottom of their profit and loss statement every so often, and if the bottom figure is not a negative number, they think they are OK. This is understandable since most entrepreneurs don't go into business because they love numbers. But I would always point out to my clients that "there is a long way from the top of their P&L to the bottom, and *a lot* can happen in between."

When I was consulting, the very first thing I did with a client was to figure out how to read the business's key vital signs (It's OK to groan right about now. I'll wait). I would rip apart their profit and loss statement and set it up so they could use it to manage their business. At the same time, I would put together a twelve-week cash flow management system so we could uncover any financial weaknesses that could sabotage their cash flow and threaten the business's survival.

The only other Key Performance Indicator (KPI) I would always show a client was how to calculate the breakeven point for their company. It is essential for an entrepreneur to use breakeven analysis as a tool for profit management by using what-if scenarios. If you are wondering what breakeven formula I was using, it was: *Breakeven = Fixed expense ÷ (1 − [Variable Cost ÷ Sales])*. Sorry! I almost forgot. This book is not a how-to book on entrepreneurship.

Entrepreneurs don't fail because they lack profits on their financial documents. They go out of business because they don't manage their cash and can't pay their bills. When you're on the entrepreneur detour, it's easier to avoid roadside bombs when you can see them up ahead—before you actually drive over them and they explode.

> "When you're on the entrepreneur detour, it's easier to avoid any roadside bombs when you can see them up ahead."
>
> @realKevinCortez #EmbraceTheDetour

Just like the rest of life, entrepreneurs must make choices. One of the most important choices they should make is to gain some *financial intelligence* and manage their cash tightly. If they don't, they will eventually be blindsided. Ouch!

I would always make sure my consulting clients understood that having tighter cash controls actually improved their profits. How? By being aware of how your expenses affected the net profit. For example, did you know that by cutting your expenses by 10 percent, you can increase your bottom-line profit by as much as 50 percent?

This is because as businesses grow, most entrepreneurs are focused on the big picture, such as top-line revenue growth, and they don't understand that expenses can spiral out of control. Many of these expenses can easily be cut as they are not critical to servicing your customers or growing your business. How many believe what I just said?

DANGER AHEAD

I can't stress enough how important it is for entrepreneurs to know when their financial data seems out of whack. In essence, that is what gives you a very clear picture of what's working and not working in your business financially. When financial controls are not in place, it's just a catastrophe waiting to happen.

I'm still haunted by the disturbing call I received from a wonderful man who had a trucking company in California. I had really enjoyed working with this Russian immigrant who was living the American dream. When he arrived in the United States, he started driving a big rig, and now he owned a fleet of twenty semi-trucks. He and his sweet wife had been able to purchase a nice home and were raising a couple of beautiful young daughters. This guy was also one of those bigger-than-life characters whom you just knew not to mess with. When his booming voice would bark out orders in Russian, everyone in the office would snap to it.

It had been a while since I had spent time in his business, trying to help him get a handle on everything. Now, as I listened to him on the other end of the phone, he was telling me how he had just lost everything. He was sobbing inconsolably as he tried to explain what had happened. My heart really went out to him, but at that point, there was nothing I could do to help. It was upsetting because I knew for a fact he could have saved his business.

What happened? When I had arrived at his company eighteen months earlier, he was managing the business out of his checkbook. His business was an all-but-Red Cross-declared disaster zone. Hundreds of thousands of dollars were flying all over the place. Worse, he was "factoring" his account receivables. If you're not familiar with that term, it's when a business sells its receivables (i.e., invoices) to a third party (called a factor) at a discount to raise capital. The factor then collects payment on those invoices from the business's customers. In my opinion, factoring is always bad news. It can become like a big bowl of crack for a business owner.

I immediately found a Certified QuickBooks ProAdvisor in the area to come into the business and set up an accounting system. Once we got all of the financial information entered into the software, I was able to set up a flex budget and cash flow management system. Before I suspended the consulting project, I showed them everything they needed to do so they could get their finances in order. I warned them they were going to have to make some difficult choices and that pain would be involved. I emphasized that it would require a strong commitment to drastically cut back on any unnecessary expenses, but these actions would help them be successful in the future.

Did they heed my warning? Sadly, no.

Did they tighten their spending belt? Again, no.

Did they follow the plan I had laid out for their business? Nope ... and they lost it all.

I wish I could say this story was the exception, but over half of the companies I tried to help are no longer in existence. Every company that went out of business has a similar gut-wrenching story attached to it.

Thankfully, this is not the case for every past client. Several of the businesses I spent time helping are still going strong. What is the difference between the two? In general, the entrepreneurs who failed didn't understand how to manage their financial foundation, while those who succeeded did.

When the owner of the trucking company saw a lot of money coming into his business, he didn't know that most of it needed to be invested back into the company. When he invited me to dinner at his home, he proudly showed off the $60,000 ruby chandelier he had imported from Russia. When I looked at it, all I could think of was how much gas he could have purchased for his trucks. I cringed when he told me how he'd rented a helicopter to fly his young daughter to a local park where they were having her birthday party. As I listened, I thought of how the money spent on a helicopter should have been directed toward less factoring.

When an entrepreneur starts out, they usually have no choice but to watch every penny. But as revenue starts to increase, things can go sideways in a hurry. Now, there are more choices as to where the money can go. And if you're not careful, you can justify it going to things that are not in the best interest of the business (e.g., finding its way into your personal bank account instead). This was never more on display than on the last management consulting engagement I had before transitioning into what I'm currently doing.

Two gentlemen had just started a TV media buying agency. One partner was an all-star salesman, and the other was a strong admin guy. They hired me to work with them exclusively, and over the next two years I devoted myself full-time to helping their company become successful. I developed the entire infrastructure, including the management, operational, and financial sides of the agency. My job was to increase profitability and keep track of all the moving parts. Our focused efforts drove rapid growth to the low eight figures in annual revenues in two short years.

This could have been an absolutely top-shelf business, but there was just one problem: both owners had an insatiable desire for money. I'm not trying to impugn anyone; I'm simply trying to set the table. I had set up an incredibly generous payout structure for them based on a percentage of net revenue. But every time I turned around, our bookkeeper was having to transfer additional funds into their personal bank accounts. Needless to say, the amounts were way above my recommended percentage.

These profit distributions were beyond excessive. I didn't begrudge them for wanting to spend a lot of money on stuff, but did they both really need those private jets? (You read that correctly.) Anyhow, as the greed began to catch up to the owners, it became apparent that they needed to cut back on their spending.

Having worked with them so closely, I saw the writing on the wall. I knew they would soon be taking an ax to the business's expenses (including my fees) so they wouldn't have to cut back on their personal income. I left on good terms. A year and a half later, their business could no longer act as their personal piggy bank, and they had to close up shop. Sheesh, what a shame!

That last consulting engagement ended in 2010, and the economy had not yet recovered from the 2008 financial crisis. I had a feeling that small business owners were not in the mood to pay for a management consultant to help them in their businesses so soon after the economic meltdown. I wasn't quite sure what was next for me. Not to be overly dramatic, but that's not a comfortable place to be when you're fifty years old and out of a job.

FOLLOW YOUR EFFORT, NOT YOUR PASSION

There is a lot of talk about "following your passion," especially at graduation ceremonies, but that would not have been the best advice for me. I was passionate about Brazilian Jiu-Jitsu at the time, but that would not have been the best thing to follow at that point in my life. Ya think? Actually, now that we're on the subject, I believe we should *not* follow our passion, but we should bring our passion to everything we do.

I knew the only things I had absolute control over were my attitude and the effort I could put forth toward something. Our effort and attitude are the only things we can control. Everything else is dependent on several other outside factors. I needed to find something I could focus on that I wouldn't mind expending a great deal of time and effort on.

I looked at what I enjoyed doing in the job world, and it was obvious to me that I liked marketing and brand development more than anything else. Why? Because it is fun, and I'm good at it. Have you ever noticed that if you find something extremely enjoyable, you will spend the time necessary to become relatively good at it?

"The only things we have control over are our attitude and our effort."

@realKevinCortez #EmbraceTheDetour

It was May 2010, and I was reading about Google's new mobile-first rule. On February 16, 2010, during a keynote at the Mobile World Congress in Barcelona, Google chief executive Eric Schmidt announced the idea of "Mobile First."

He explained that everything Google is now doing is being created with mobile in mind: "We understand that the new rule is mobile first. ... Mobile first in everything."[8]

When I heard this, I connected some dots immediately. In a mobile-first world, marketers have the opportunity to be highly relevant by considering a consumer's intent, context, and immediacy.

I knew it would only be a matter of time before "Mobile First" would become "Mobile Always."

When this hit my radar, I thought, *Entrepreneurs are going to need help with this mobile marketing thing.*

That was my eureka moment.

I started my digital marketing agency, Mobile Marketing Helper, that day.

I immediately went to GoDaddy's website and purchased the domain name MobileMarketingHelper.com for $19.95.

Then I ordered a worthless sixty-seven-dollar Mobile Marketing Course from one of those *Internet gurus* who said he had "cracked the code."

Once again, I was off to *#EmbraceTheDetour*.

Chapter Reflections

What are your thoughts? I would love for you to share some of your answers to these questions on any of my social media platforms. Go to "KevinCortez.com" and link to them from there.

1. When I mentioned that the way I emotionally handled the brutal stress of being a business consultant was to look at it as though I was "getting paid to learn," did that resonate with you? Have you had periods in your life where you got paid to learn? What were the results?

2. If you have a business, have you bothered to gain an understanding of how to look at your financial indicators?

3. As I mentioned, the only things I believe we have control over are our attitude and our effort. Looking honestly at your life, how is your attitude doing these days? What about the amount of effort you are putting forth?

Scan the QR code for bonus content.

CHAPTER 6

The Economy
of an Entrepreneur

" **Y**our interview has been scheduled for Wednesday, May 9, 2012, at 1:00 p.m. with our Senior Director of Digital Guest Experience." That was the first sentence of the email sent to me from the largest chain in the convenience retailing industry, with annual revenues of over $84 billion. (That's a billion with a *b*.)

A high-powered recruiter named Ginger had called me a couple of weeks previously to see if I would be interested in a position that would head up the mobile marketing department of a major company that had more stores than McDonald's. She said the role would be "responsible for lifecycle management of new mobile commerce products to include assessing, defining, prioritizing, designing and executing." Don't you just love corporate multisyllabic jargon? I guess they wanted a geek to help them offer "transformational, granular deliverables."

I told her, "Of course I'm interested in checking this opportunity out." Wouldn't you have if you were me?

Ginger and I prepared an executive summary of my background, and she sent it off.

This corporation was moving its mobile marketing from an outside media agency into a newly formed division within the company. I don't want to mention who this corporation was, but let's just say they changed their name in 1946 to reflect their new extended hours: 7 a.m. to 11 p.m.

I put on my favorite Giorgio Armani suit and went for my interview. I was led into a beautiful, glass-walled conference room. As I sat in one of the twenty chairs around a ginormous table, the interviewer began to go on and on about how he was a "disrupter" and that he had been looking forward to showing me some of their plans for this new mobile marketing division. I remember Mr. Disrupter asking me if I had read *The Innovator's Dilemma* because that was the thesis of his approach to business. I hadn't, but I wrote down the book's title to show him I was paying attention.

He went through a super fancy presentation deck he had put together for his higher-ups. They were going to spend over $3.5 million on mobile marketing within the next few months, and he was in charge of getting the project up and running.

After he was done dazzling me with how they were going to create an app, partner with Universal Studios, and then launch promotions through QR (Quick Response) codes printed on signage and cups, he asked what I thought about the direction they were taking. He specifically wanted to know if these were the first steps I would recommend.

I had him take out his smartphone and text the word *SLURPEE* to the number 72727. He did and immediately received back a text that read, "Show this text inside to receive your FREE Slurpee. Tap the following link for more info and specials." When he tapped the link, a simple mobile website landing page opened on his phone with all kinds of cool info, a video, social share buttons, and directions on how to add the 7-Eleven logo icon to the screen of his smartphone.

I told Mr. Disrupter I had a lot of experience in the "C-Store" world since I had run a beverage distributorship. I said that creating a path to purchase (see how I used current buzzwords right there?) would be simple. With this call-to-action, you could place signs at the gas pumps so that people would go inside the store for their Slurpee after purchasing gas. And naturally, once they were in the store, they would see other products they wanted to buy.

The franchisees who owned the stores would love this campaign because it was simple to execute at the store-level, and they would now have a way to send out text campaigns once every four to six weeks to bring customers back into the store. This would help drive top-line revenue for their businesses, which was the end game, right? Then, to close the deal, I told him that "interaction is much more important than innovation."

I wasn't expecting what happened next. I was shocked and caught totally off guard. Mr. Disrupter just stared at me with this strange look on his face. After a long pause, he eventually said, "We can't do that."

I said, "Why wouldn't you be able to do this?"

His reply was, "We would have to move the Mobile Marketing Department into the *Marketing* Division."

Now I was the one with a strange look on my face. Out of curiosity, I just had to ask, "What department is it in now?"

He answered, "The Technology Division."

Seriously? I thought that but didn't say it because I could tell he was committed to his mobile marketing approach.

It didn't matter that I had run hundreds of marketing campaigns of this type while he was theorizing about being a disrupter after reading some book. Apparently, he thought they only needed a full-on techie who could write programming code for their new app. He just figured that's how mobile marketing worked. Needless to say, we were not a fit.

If Mr. Disrupter had only listened to what I shared with him, he might have been the hero who saved his company millions of dollars.

How can I be so sure?

Two years later, I pulled into one of their stores by my house to get some gas, and what do you think I saw as I reached for the gas pump handle? That's right. I saw a sign that read, "Text *SLURPEE* to 711711 for a FREE Slurpee."

I smiled as I got my phone out and opted into the campaign. And when I got a text back, my smile got really big. What I saw was the marketing campaign I had recommended two years earlier. Was I upset? Not even a little. Why not? Read on.

THE ADVANTAGE OF BEING SMALL

My experience with such a large corporation should greatly encourage every small business owner. I want you to recognize that technology is changing so fast that the big companies can't adapt to it like small business owners can. In the current economy, entrepreneurs can change what they're doing much quicker. This is a tremendous advantage over the big competition, which are slow, bureaucratic, and entrenched.

I'm always explaining to entrepreneurs that most marketing incorporates three things: strategy, technology, and execution. If you own a business, don't get all caught up in the changing technology. Always focus on finding out what the best strategy is, and then apply that strategy with excellence to whatever technology is out there.

When I started running text marketing campaigns in 2010 for example, only a few business owners thought they would be effective. Some were even *hostile* to the idea. They would tell me all the reasons (excuses) as to why it wouldn't work. Sigh. Fortunately, I had other digital marketing services that they did want (e.g., website design and online marketing services).

My clients who started integrating that type of marketing now enjoy a massive advantage over those who didn't understand what was happening back then. These early adopters figured out what worked for their particular business and what didn't. They have built up a loyal database of customers whom they can interact with through various types of SMS (text) marketing and social media campaigns.

I now have businesses contacting our agency, wanting me to help them break into that marketing environment. Since they are now a few years behind, they have to play catch-up. Also, they are competing against those that have been doing it for a while as well as the more prominent brands that are starting to figure things out. Now, everybody knows it's important to incorporate "mobile" into their marketing mix. Oh well. Better late than never.

WHAT WAS OLD IS NEW AGAIN

A while back, my friend Kurt texted me, "Look what I found." He had attached a photo he had just taken at the Laws Railroad Museum located just outside my hometown of Bishop. The photo featured the McNally family going back six generations, and there I was, a picture of me in high school titled "Kevin James Cortez – 5th Generation."

I previously mentioned that I'd grown up in a small town, but just to give you a better idea of how small, I was in my early teens before we got our second traffic light. The total surrounding population was around ten thousand (if you counted bugs). By the way, it's still that same size.

Since the closest city, Reno, was over two hundred miles away, "buying local" was our only choice. As you might imagine, everybody knew everybody. If I ever did something wrong, my parents would find out about it before I'd even get home.

A majority of the business owners in the community had lived there for most of their lives. And since they would run into residents everywhere they went, they treated each other with respect and courtesy (even when they didn't want to). These entrepreneurs understood that they depended upon what the small community said about them. Word of mouth was *everything*!

I remember that as I got older, our family would periodically take the three-and-a-half-hour car ride to Reno to shop. Why? Because they could save money by purchasing products outside of our community. My parents pointed out to me that some of our hometown business owners were taking advantage of the fact that they had a captive audience.

All that changed when Kmart came to town and many of the local retailers were thrown into turmoil. Businesses that had been there for generations got trampled by the low prices and found it nearly impossible to compete.

But here's what I want to point out: some survived. The businesses that withstood the giant retailer setting up shop were the ones that had built authentic relationships with their customers. They had not taken them for granted, and they had kept close personal and business ties with the community. Their loyal customers didn't mind paying a little more for genuine caring … and excellent customer service.

As the years progressed, in general, consumers everywhere began to reject the notion that customer service had value and businesses no longer had to be "relational." It was all about making the transaction and improving the bottom line. Sadly, we all became disconnected because of this.

Then the Internet hit the scene, and by the mid-1990s it had become fully commercialized. This made things even worse as we became even more isolated. Now, many businesses didn't have to worry about word of mouth and some even set up ways to avoid directly dealing with customers. Phone numbers disappeared from websites, and if you did finally find a number to call, it was hard to communicate with the foreigner on the other end of the line because they were reading from some weird script. Terrible service, unfair practices, and indifference became the norm. Do you like it when you feel depersonalized, isolated, and ignored? Me either.

Fortunately, the second stage of World Wide Web development, called Web 2.0, showed up around 2004. It was especially characterized by the change from static web pages to user-generated content and the growth of social media. This connected us in a totally small-town way. The bottom line, now people were able to talk to one another again, in real-time. What did this mean for businesses? "Word of mouth" was back. Customers are now active participants in companies and brands, influencing company strategy arm-in-arm with CEOs.

I absolutely love this change! I already think like an old-fashioned, small-town business owner, and so should you if you're an entrepreneur. Hopefully, you already extend ethics and manners, actual manners, to your customers. If you don't authentically care about every person you do business with, you will lose in the long run. Authenticity and transparency are everything!

While big companies are having to worry about their shareholders, stock prices, and quarterly numbers, we can put our effort into getting to know our consumers better. As large businesses focus on short-term results to make their bonuses, we can create better marketing to get consumers' attention so they are more likely to buy from us. Why? Because we actually care.

And for crying out loud, put a phone number on your website and have the phone answered when someone calls.

NEW ECONOMIC REALITY

One by one, in a brightly lit conference room, I listened as everyone introduced themselves. These corporate lawyers, controllers, marketing executives, and commercial bankers, all from the secure suburbs of north Dallas, were all "in transition" (the nice term for being out of work). The group met on Monday mornings to provide structure for the week. Throughout the meeting, I listened to those who had gone to premier MBA programs, guided companies through multimillion-dollar decisions, and had held previous titles like Chief Financial Officer, Treasurer, and Vice President of Marketing.

When I was there, they talked about how their days were filled with a revolving door of networking meetings, applications, and chasing down the all-important (but elusive) hiring "decision-maker" at their target companies. Some asked if they could practice their elevator pitches with someone, while others wanted help editing their resumes. I noticed a few even exchanged job leads and LinkedIn tips. But the most valuable interaction I saw that morning was the emotional support they provided one another.

Being unemployed is the worst! When you lose your job, you also lose a significant component of your identity, along with your daily routines and financial security. Job loss and unemployment can upend our feelings of self-worth, comfort, security, and personal control. If you have ever experienced losing a job, did you feel rejected, defeated, demoralized, disoriented, or worthless? Those feelings sure can be scary. I know from experience.

The emotions job seekers experience, while normal in context, can spiral into paralyzing depression. Mental health experts say negative, self-defeating thoughts take over people's minds and govern their behavior. People overeat or undereat or sleep too much or too little. When depression sets in, conducting a job search and crawling out of unemployment grow even harder.

Support groups like the one I observed that day have sprung up all over the country as millions of talented people have struggled with the fact that the world has changed. After the 2008 financial crisis (which pushed, at the peak, 15 million Americans out of work[9]), we went through the longest, and by most measures worst, economic recession since the Great Depression. Even now, in the current economic environment, it's a mistake to think that the job market has not changed big-time. If you don't acknowledge this new economic reality, you are in for some serious trauma if you ever find yourself out of work.

All I could think about during my time with these sharp individuals was that they needed to adjust their thinking. A year and a half previously, I had also found myself out of a job and looking at a résumé brimming with accomplishments.

At that time, when I was also unemployed, everyone was complaining about the "Great Recession" that was upon us. Yes, we were all dumbfounded by our inability to land a position. Nobody was immune to the punch in the mouth that came with the shock of finding ourselves suddenly tossed onto the employment rubbish heap (just when we felt on top of our game). Every one of us was living the same nightmare haunting millions of Americans.

But I remember thinking about how more millionaires were created as a result of the Great Depression than in any other period in American history. Opportunities that were not present before suddenly became available. Innovative entrepreneurs edged in and positioned themselves for when the economic climate improved. That's what I tried to remind myself.

An economic downturn can actually be a good time to start a business: you have time to get the business fundamentals right and test your business model. Great Depression entrepreneurs made the best of the crisis to provide a service, or product, for new markets. This was one of the things that motivated me to start my media agency, Mobile Marketing Helper.

The mobile marketing space was (and still is) very fragmented. It's like the Wild Wild West, as marketers are shooting off promotional campaigns in every direction. Fortunately, it didn't take me too long to create a viable business model that was soon generating substantial top-line revenue growth for me. Whew!

Then, about a year into running my agency, I recognized the incredible opportunity to franchise the company. A few of my competitors said they were "like a franchise," but they had not created an actual franchise business model. So, I took my twenty-plus years of experience serving the small-to-medium-size-enterprise (SME) sector, created the Mobile Marketing Business Development Model, and made it available to franchisees. It was designed to provide suitable business professionals with a framework for developing independent digital marketing advisory practices directed specifically at SMEs.

This was why I was at that Monday morning networking meeting for those *corporate refugees* who were "in transition." I figured that if someone there was a fit, I could offer them an opportunity to change the direction of their life. I assumed that some of them had entrepreneurial dreams, and I wanted to offer a way for them to transform that dream of business ownership into a here-and-now reality by owning one of the first mobile marketing franchises.

Several franchise brokers whom I showed what I had put together for my potential franchisees absolutely loved the concept. I was told they thought it was among the best in the business services category. These individual brokers immediately started recommending my opportunity to their prequalified prospective franchise buyers. Soon, I was going over my franchise disclosure document and online training materials with several potential business partners.

Everyone I talked to had impressive professional achievements and credentials, but there was one problem: not one of them was an entrepreneur. Even though they had the $15,000 franchise fee and wanted to start a home-based marketing business, I just knew they would fail. How did I know? Because, from what I could tell, everyone I talked to had been used to working at a job where they told everyone else what to do.

It was clear that they were not willing to humble themselves and actually do the work it would take to succeed. I had naively thought they understood that when you ran your own business, success didn't just magically happen. I could have just taken their money, but that would have been plain wrong on my part.

Can you tell I was disappointed that this detour led to a dead end? I had spent a lot of time, money, and effort putting an opportunity together that I thought could help those who had generally excelled at what they had done previously but had been laid off late in their careers.

Thankfully, all was not lost in what I had done. I organized some of what I had put together and created a reseller program. The program was designed for those individuals who wanted to sell our services (in addition to whatever else they were doing), and we would "revenue share" whatever services they sold. It has worked out for several entrepreneurs who were willing to have a side hustle. This was just one more example of me having to *#EmbraceTheDetour*.

Chapter Reflections

What are your thoughts? I would love for you to share some of your answers to these questions on any of my social media platforms. Go to "KevinCortez.com" and link to them from there.

1. My experience with big corporations has shown me that being small is an advantage because of our flexibility and speed of implementation. Is there an opportunity in your industry you could take advantage of?

2. Reflect on my statement: "If you don't authentically care about every person you do business with, you will lose in the long run." How does that statement affect the need for changes in your life?

3. When I shared my emotions that went along with being unemployed, did that help you better understand how those feelings can be so scary? Do you know anyone who may be experiencing that pain? If so, have you reached out to them and encouraged them in any way?

Scan the QR code for bonus content.

CHAPTER 7

The Relationships of an Entrepreneur

While running our family business in California, I authored a couple of Christian books that were distributed in over thirty countries. As a result, I was asked to speak at various places. At a leadership conference in the Philippines, I was having dinner with a small group, and a young man sitting next to me asked a great question:

"What is the one thing you've learned that has helped you in life more than anything else?"

I replied, "My understanding and acceptance that people are a trip."

He immediately laughed because he knew exactly what I was referring to. The complexity of individuals and their unpredictability is true in every culture. Human nature is a fascinating thing. Just when you think someone is going to behave a certain way, they will surprise you and act completely different from what you expected. So, sometimes it can be challenging to relate and interact with others. And if you're in business, you will need to get along with others, including those who can be difficult at times. You know the type.

All of us have been given a most valuable gift—a free will—which comes into play with the choices we make. Have you ever been shocked by something someone did? Or, more importantly, have you ever been surprised by something *you* did? I have.

Sometimes we make good choices; sometimes we don't. What's really a bummer is when someone else's bad choice negatively affects our lives. Oof. We would prefer to be surrounded by people who are helpful and encouraging all the time, but that is simply not going to be our everyday experience. There will always be those in our lives who can be a source of angst, tumult, and chaos.

We like to categorize people into two groups: the ones we like and those we don't. While our personal preferences factor into who we like as friends, we must make a distinction between our professional and personal relationships.

First, our professional life is not the setting for establishing close friendships. The marketplace, especially in today's environment, will include many different cultures, ethnic groups, religions, political affiliations, and sexual orientations. Thus, we have to interact with people we might not relate to on a personal level. That is why we must develop a professional attitude as entrepreneurs, one in which our personal opinions don't taint everything.

Staying "professional" requires focus. We must focus on making sure we are treating everyone with respect and appreciation. Do you think this takes some discipline and self-control with certain people? Oh, a-a-absolutely!

When I cross swords with someone, I try not to take things personally. I know it's hard when our emotions flare up. We are tempted to respond by lashing out or retaliating. But we must keep our eyes on the endgame and not let how we *feel* get the best of us. If we react incorrectly to the brouhaha, we could miss out on some incredible business opportunities down the road.

Naturally, we gravitate to those people with whom we share some common interests, but we should still enjoy others with whom we don't have much in common. I am grateful for those in my life who don't think as I think. I appreciate those with different personality gifts than me— especially other entrepreneurs.

You don't want to be judged and dismissed for your personal beliefs, lifestyle, or class, do you? Then embrace the true meaning of acceptance and tolerance. I found that doing this has also helped with my patience and compassion. As you look around at all the different personalities and temperaments in your professional life, I encourage you to be thankful.

IT'S ABOUT PEOPLE

In case I haven't made it crystal clear by now, then what I'm about to say next is for you. Ready? Pay close attention. Here it is again:

If you are an entrepreneur, your relationships with others are extremely important!

This can be essential when it comes to connecting with other entrepreneurs. One of the first steps I took after launching my media agency was to get myself around other business owners in Dallas. I knew that isolated entrepreneurs are far more vulnerable to failure than those who are unified in purpose. Being an entrepreneur is lonely. When you unify with other entrepreneurs around the purpose of growing your business, you will experience tremendous benefits.

"Isolated entrepreneurs are far more vulnerable to failure than those who are unified in purpose."

@realKevinCortez #EmbraceTheDetour

I pursued entrepreneurial relationships by joining a local networking group of independent business people who met at the nearby Original Pancake House every Wednesday morning at 7:45. The express purpose of our time together was not to eat breakfast but to get to know one another and pass business referrals. It was structured in such a way that required us to meet with others from the group outside of the weekly meetings so we could develop more meaningful relationships.

In reality, most companies have similar business models, which means they also have similar challenges. In my experience, I have found that most problems entrepreneurs encounter are not unique to one industry, business, or owner. So, I knew that if I were to make a commitment to hang around other entrepreneurs on a weekly basis, being accountable would help my emotional state of mind. I also knew that since the others in the group were making the same commitment to show up every week like I was, there was a better chance for genuine relationships to form.

At the beginning of each of our meetings, the person leading would ask, "How is everybody doing today?"

Everyone would answer in unison, "Livin' the dream."

Then the leader would ask, "And why are we here?"

The members would answer, "To make money!"

But this was *not* why I had joined the group. I understood that the group could be a steady source of qualified business referrals for some members, and I received additional business because of my involvement, but I also acknowledged a simple reality: the moment we left the meeting at 9:30 a.m., no one in that room would think about me until they saw me the following Wednesday morning. And that was OK.

It wasn't that they didn't necessarily care about me and my business. They were busy with their lives, i.e., they had a lot on their minds. Can we agree that life is relentless? So, I knew not to rely on their referrals to grow my business.

From my perspective, just because someone likes you and your business doesn't mean they have a responsibility to pass on your information. I really appreciate referrals, and I don't mind asking for them, but I know that the success of my business is my sole responsibility. If my service offerings come up in the course of someone's conversation, great. But if they don't, that's fine too.

Because I don't put any of my expectations on others, I don't get disappointed (or mad) when others are not measuring up to a standard I was hoping they would meet. When interacting with others, I believe it's a good idea not to expect *anything* from them. I try to exchange my expectations of them with a simple appreciation of who they are as a person. I genuinely appreciate any attention they may give me because I respect how important their time is.

Let's look at it a little differently. Are you an entrepreneur who needs some financial resources to move your business forward? Have you had to downsize your entrepreneurial dream because you lack money? If that's the case, I believe it may not be all about your lack of resources. I would suggest it may actually be about your lack of resourcefulness.

"It's not about your resources. It's about your resourcefulness."

@realKevinCortez #EmbraceTheDetour

What do I mean by that? It is not about your bank account balance but your ability to come up with other ways to win. And those "other ways" usually involve your access to information and/or people. What information do you need to learn? Who else do you know who can help you in your situation? You are one relationship away from changing the entire future of your business.

It is essential to spend time with other entrepreneurs and talk about the challenges we all face. We are on the same battlefield, and we've experienced things that only other entrepreneurs will ever understand. Thus, those relationships may have precisely what you need (and you don't even realize it).

I don't know about you, but it has helped me to walk with others on this crazy journey. I've found that the emotional strength it brings can be more important than actual financial strength.

I see so many entrepreneurs get so caught up in the *transactional* aspect of business that they miss the *relational* part. Because I believe that the transaction is not the most important part, I want every interaction I have with someone to be primarily *relational*, not *transactional*.

RELATIONSHIP LEVELS

Like you, I interact with a lot of different people on different levels. I am aware that some of these relationships are personal, some are professional, and a select few are both. My goal is to interact with everyone in such a way that it feels completely personal because I truly do care for people on an individual level.

I have found it helpful to divide my relationships into three levels:

1. face-to-face
2. shoulder-to-shoulder
3. back-to-back

All our relationships start at a foundational level. You may know one another, but only on the surface. I refer to these types of relationships as *face-to-face*. At this level, we may only interact with these individuals on occasion, but when we do, there is some sort of connection there.

We interact with our face-to-face relationships on a level whereby we communicate with them directly, but not on a very personal level. We have a genuine relationship but are not necessarily "doing life" with them. This could include business relationships, social media relationships, work relationships, and people we may have just met.

The second level of relationships describes those that are substantive and continuing. I think of these people in my life as *shoulder-to-shoulder* friendships. I know we are walking through life together, side-by-side (shoulder-to-shoulder), and if one of us eats the pavement, the other is there to reach out and help us get back up. Do you have any shoulder-to-shoulder relationships you can lean on when the going gets tough? I hope so. We all need support from friends when situations get sketchy.

Lastly, there are those rare relationships on a level that can be referred to as *back-to-back*. These are those friendships that became established through extended face-to-face interactions. Then the relationship is able to transition into a deeper, shoulder-to-shoulder experience. And now, there is a level of trust that enables the friendship to go back-to-back: you now have each other's back, and you will not hesitate to defend each other no matter what life throws at you.

How can you tell if a relationship has reached this level? Simple. Have you ever felt like you've been in a train wreck that sailed over a cliff in the middle of a hurricane, only to be struck by lightning as soon as you exited the train? Was your friend with you throughout every terrible moment?

I am so thankful I have a couple of friendships at this level. Those relationships have withstood the junk that life can throw at us. No matter what goes down, we always have each other's backs.

CROWDS AND TRIBES

In 2016, my media agency was one of the main sponsors of the Small Business Expo in Houston, Texas. These trade shows are the nation's largest business-to-business conferences and networking events of their kind. In addition to having a premium booth, my business was highlighted on all the marketing collateral. I even had my logo prominently displayed on the photo backdrop for the event, where everybody posed for their photo op.

Since I was also a featured speaker at one of the Business Critical Workshops, I had been told by the person who had recommended the sponsorship package to me that "this event is going to be an absolute game-changer" for my business. I had gone to a few of these expos as an attendee in the past, so I knew that it wouldn't be as big of a deal as I was told, but I did think it was going to be helpful.

What I didn't know (until a few days before the event) was that several former *Shark Tank* contestants would be participating in a panel discussion at the same time as my workshop. Now, would you rather listen to some guy you've never heard of talk about marketing or hear stories about what it was like to be a participant on *Shark Tank*?

Umm, me too.

That wasn't even the worst part. What made matters unbearable were the logistics of my workshop. The *Shark Tank* discussion was only about fifty feet away from the area where I was speaking. Because our stages were only separated by thin curtains, the sound from their speakers drowned out my dinky, little sound system. It was soooo bad. Those who were listening to me found it almost impossible to focus on all the awe-inspiring things I was saying. Argh! All was not lost. At least I can tell you about another entrepreneur detour I ended up on, right?

Actually, there was another thing that happened to me that day in Houston that was a defining moment in my entrepreneur journey: I realized that although I was surrounded by a crowd of small-business owners, and I was interacting with several of them throughout the event, I did not feel connected to any of them. I always like being around that type of crowd and talking with various business owners, but this day felt different.

It's hard to explain, but that whole experience bugged me—a lot. When I thought about how I was feeling over the next several weeks, I concluded that there was, in fact, an important distinction between a *crowd* and a *tribe* that I needed to address. When I stepped back and looked at it, I had not yet found my tribe in the world of entrepreneurs. That's why, when I would interact with various groups of business owners, it would always seem like I was zigging while everyone else was zagging.

Have you ever felt alone in a crowd?

Seth Godin, the guy who coined the term *permission marketing* back in the 1990s, wrote a book called *Tribes*. In this context, he defines a tribe as "a group of people connected to one another, connected to a leader, and connected to an idea."[10] I like that concept.

"There is an important distinction between a crowd and a tribe."

@realKevinCortez #EmbraceTheDetour

We can be connected to various tribes (groups of like-minded people) in the different areas of our lives, e.g., tribes based on business, ethnicity, religion, politics, or something like music—think of the Deadheads. I was connected to like-minded people in other areas of my life, but in business, not so much.

CAFFEINE, CHAOS, AND CUSSING

Over the next several months, I began to pay closer attention to who was doing what in the land of entrepreneurs. Since I wasn't up to speed on what was going on with the Who's Who in the thought-leader zoo, I didn't know who was popular and who wasn't. As the weeks turned into months, it appeared that I hadn't missed much: everyone I listened to or read was saying pretty much the same basic things that had been around for decades. Of course, if I wanted to learn about their really good stuff, I could always find their most valuable advice behind their online paywall. That is, I could pay some serious money for access to their best content.

Oh, there was one thing I noticed that I found striking: several of the entrepreneurs who were being put up on a pedestal had yet to make a profit in their businesses. One brilliant entrepreneur was particularly fascinating to me: Elon Musk. In 2013, he was the highest paid CEO in the world according to *Time* magazine.[11] This visionary has built a multibillion-dollar fortune running companies that make electric cars, sell solar panels, and launch rockets into space, and he has not even come close to showing a profit in any of these companies.[12] Ever. These businesses are subsidized.

None of what Mr. Musk is doing is sustainable without some entity willing to give him well over $5 billion. By the way, I have no animus against this entrepreneurial icon one way or the other. My reason for pointing this out to you is so you won't compare your entrepreneur journey to some of these entrepreneurs in the limelight. Besides, if your combined businesses are underwritten to the tune of $5 billion by the government, I'm pretty sure you would at least be showing a profit. Do you agree?

As 2016 was coming to a close, I was watching an online video that one of my competitors had posted on his Facebook business page. He was all excited about an interview he had just done with a guy named Gary Vaynerchuk. I had never heard of Gary Vee, another name he goes by, but by the time this video finished, I realized I was listening to someone with whom I felt a connection.

Eighty-seven percent of what Gary said were things that I say but with different word choices, and he communicated in a much more entertaining way than I do. It was so refreshing to listen to someone who was like-minded and that I could relate to. He was actually running his companies (and they were making a profit). He had even previously worked in his family's liquor business.

After watching that eighteen-minute video, I couldn't wait to try and find more information about this dude. It took me 0.025 seconds. Seriously. His content was *everywhere*!

What I found even more amazing was that his best stuff was not reserved for those who purchased it. It was all free. I was surprised I hadn't heard of him before because he is one popular somebody!

When I first started watching Gary's daily vlog series called "DailyVee," I thought he should rename it "Caffeine, Chaos, and Cussing." He moves through life with a coffee cup in hand at a speed that would cause most of us whiplash. And there appears to be chaos all around him. But if you know what to look for, everything is actually very orderly. As for the cussing part, Gary uses the f-word like Michelangelo used a chisel. That's just the way he chooses to communicate. And it definitely works for him.

You may wonder what it is that has brought so many people into this man's entrepreneurial *tribe*. I can't speak for others, but I would guess it is his *authenticity*.

Everyone is desperate for authenticity—in business and in real life, in work and in play. I think we are attracted to it because it's in such short supply. Consequently, when we see it, we'll wait for it. We'll watch it on Internet videos. We'll stand in line for a chance to be near it. Fans, entrepreneurs, rappers—we know authenticity when we see it, even if we're not looking for it. And Gary Vaynerchuk has authenticity in spades.

I've never met him. However, I know him enough through his daily video blog series and the #AskGaryVee show to know that he's simply a flawed human who is decent, kind, and one gifted entrepreneur.

Even though I like Gary, I can't recommend that you take his advice on "life" … but I do think you can learn branding and entrepreneurship from him.

If Gary is not your cup of tea, you may want to check out Tom Bilyeu or Marie Forleo. I also found these entrepreneurs to be authentic and inspiring (although I can't endorse how they approach "life" overall, either).

If you want to know who I can recommend regarding advice on how to best approach life, check out author John Bevere or Pastor Charles Nieman. I know these two men personally, and they have helped me tremendously.

Here's the thing: it can be more valuable for you to watch the behavior of someone who is winning at what you want to be doing than to simply listen to (or read) what they are saying. Some things cannot be taught; they must be caught. If you know what to be open for, you can catch what they are doing and apply it to your life.

"Some things cannot be taught; they must be caught."

@realKevinCortez #EmbraceTheDetour

This book is an example of me applying what you just read. As I watched Vaynerchuk, it became obvious almost immediately that he is the walking definition of a good entrepreneur. When I saw how he put forth such tremendous effort into building his personal brand, I caught how important this must be.

How did I know I caught it? Because I was moved to action: I decided that 2017 was going to be the year I focused on establishing my personal brand, and this book would be the cornerstone of that effort.

I figured the first step was to document some of my entrepreneurial journey and put myself out there on a platform I'm familiar with: the written word. So here we are.

I have intentionally tried to make this book about my behavior during the unexpected twists and turns in becoming an entrepreneur. My hope is that you will catch something that will help you succeed as you *#EmbraceTheDetour*.

Chapter Reflections

What are your thoughts? I would love for you to share some of your answers to these questions on any of my social media platforms. Go to "KevinCortez.com" and link to them from there.

1. I obviously place tremendous importance on my relationships with other entrepreneurs. If you own a business, have you placed importance on connecting with other entrepreneurs? If not, why?
2. As you examine the relationships in your life, can you clearly identify the levels you have with them?
3. Did that make sense to you when I described that some things must be caught versus taught? If not, what part was confusing?

Scan the QR code for bonus content.

CHAPTER 8

The Legacy
of an Entrepreneur

As I was waiting in the beautiful hotel lobby to be picked up for an early dinner, I thought about the group of people I would be speaking to in a couple of hours. For the last several years, I've had the honor of speaking to a few hundred men and women who were participating in a one-year residential rehabilitation program in Los Angeles. I thought about how they had become my absolute favorite assortment of people to interact with.

This particular program takes a year or longer, depending on the person's progress. In the program, individuals between the ages of eighteen and fifty-nine struggled with substance abuse, depression, anger issues, past physical and sexual abuse, and other life-controlling challenges. Picture drug addicts, gang members, criminals, prostitutes, and others who had broken lives that needed to be restored.

The men and women are housed on separate floors in the facility, but every Tuesday night everyone comes together in a group setting for a "chapel service." This meeting is typically led by their leaders or, on occasion, a guest speaker (e.g., me).

Once a year I would go and hang out with some of them during the day and then share with everyone what was on my heart that evening.

My hosts, a wonderful couple named Mike and Velma, arrived in the hotel lobby and led me out to their car. When I got into the vehicle, I was introduced to an attractive young woman named Christina. She was very put together and had the most vivacious smile. I just assumed Christina was another staff member.

As the four of us drove to the restaurant, I began to ask Christina about how she liked living in Southern California.

After some chitchat, she handed me a gift bag. When I looked in the bag, there was a cute little teddy bear and a letter addressed to me. I was a little confused … I smiled and asked, "What's this, Christina?"

She said that she had been a part of the rehabilitation program when I had visited in the past and wanted to thank me for "igniting the fire back into her heart and giving her hope."

Apparently, some things I had previously said to the group helped her tap into the courage she needed to move forward in life. I began to read her letter and became immediately overwhelmed.

Here's what it said (in part):

Dear Mr. Cortez,

My name is Christina ... and I wanted to give you my bear. Actually it's the bear that I made for my 2 year old son Malachi, at the Build-a-Bear Factory, for his birthday as a belated birthday gift.

My son means a lot to me. I haven't seen him since he was 8 months old, but I talk to him when he's around my mom. Currently my parents have guardianship of him and they live in Hawaii. But, I love my son dearly and I carry his picture with me in my notebook. So, I've been wanting to send him this bear. His name, the bear's, is Matthias ... Honestly, it is hard for me to give this bear to you but I know it's for a reason...

Oh yeah, and he talks. He says "I love you. I love you" and to me that represented God telling me that. For my son, it was to represent how much I love him ... God Bless you Mr. Cortez.

Sincerely, Christina P.

When I got done reading her letter, everything within me wanted to return her gift. Seriously, how can you even begin to come up with a price tag for what this bear meant to Christina? But I knew that, for reasons I could not comprehend, it was super important to her that she place a tangible value on the hope she had received from me at a critical time in her life. The whole experience was *extremely* humbling!

As I learned more about Christina's story over dinner, I was inspired by her courage and strength. She had overcome things that would have left most people littered along the highway of life. She had been down a very dark road that few could imagine, but now she is an incredible encouragement to others—including me.

INHERITANCE VS. LEGACY

There is a lot of talk in Entrepreneur Land about how we should go about leaving a *legacy*. Many entrepreneurs want to go beyond their company and leave a lasting tribute. The discussions around the topic of *legacy* always seem to focus on what you will leave behind when you are no longer on this earth. Some even behave like it's a competition to see how many people they can get to come to their funeral when they die.

Legacy discussions vary from, "I thought I would have figured some things out by now. What's the purpose in what I'm doing anyway?" to, "Why am I busting my butt with no end in sight?" to, "Why does it seem like I'm the only one who really cares about what this company is doing?" to the stated desire that the world be left better because of the meaningful life that was lived.

Personally, I find that many entrepreneurs confuse *inheritance* with *legacy*. Let me try to explain what I mean.

When I hear the question, "*What* is going to be your legacy?" I believe that's the wrong question to ask. The question should be, "*Who* is (present tense) your legacy?"

Inheritance is *what* you leave behind; legacy is *whom* you have impacted in a positive and meaningful way. You can purchase inheritance (e.g., money, houses, cars, stocks, and other "stuff"), but you cannot buy legacy. Your legacy is found in the people who say, "Had it not been for you, I wouldn't be where I am today."

I don't know about you, but I don't care that much about how I'm remembered in the sweet by and by. I'll be dead. I want to know what my legacy is in the nasty here and now. I'm not necessarily worried about what people will say at my funeral or what I'm going to leave behind for future generations. I want to make a positive impact on people's lives *today*.

Scan your life. Whom have you invested in? Of course, you should be investing in your family and close friendships, but what about your employees or customers? What about those other business relationships you have? Whom are you currently inspiring in some way?

If you're having a difficult time with those questions and don't know where to start, sometimes just choosing to be a positive and happy person can be an awesome gift for your relationships to receive from you. Of course, choosing to be positive can be challenging, especially in light of all the negativity that constantly bombards our minds. But what's the alternative? Choosing to be negative and miserable.

LIVE LIKE IT MATTERS

It seems as though various media outlets (on the right and the left) are slugging it out to see who can play on people's emotions to get them upset about what the other side is doing. Social media has become a hot mess of hysteria and manufactured drama that is pitting everyone against one another. At times, it's like *Lord of the Flies*, but with adults being brought to life with comments that are *extremely* divisive and polarizing. All this can be a great opportunity for us to stand out in a positive way. Be that person who goes against the grain and chooses to be happy and positive.

If you are open to legacy opportunities, you will find them happening in your life quite often. For example, when I read the following note I received after helping a multi-trade contractor in Canada, I don't necessarily feel a big sense of accomplishment:

> *Kevin, I would like to express our thanks for the successful completion of the Consulting Project that was desperately needed for the continued success of my company. You met and exceeded our expectations with the development and implementation of improvements to all aspects of our business ... We feel very fortunate to have had you involved with our company! THANKS AGAIN – John M.*

Sure, it was nice that John's business improved. But the time I spent helping him get his company back on track is *not* part of my legacy. My legacy is tied to the conversations I had with him and his family during a very difficult time when a family tragedy had just occurred.

So, this is my legacy in that instance: Two weeks before I had met John and his wife, their eldest son was driving to work in the morning and was involved in a fatal accident. As he drove over a hill, the sun was directly in his eyes, and he did not see the young woman riding her bicycle on the road until it was too late. His truck struck and killed her. The son was okay but needless to say, this accident greatly affected many people, including John and his entire family.

Since their office and workshop were integrated into their home, I was around the family the entire time. For three months, as I focused on their business, I was more concerned with wanting to have a true and meaningful impact during that very tough time for their family. I wanted to be sensitive to what was transpiring in everyone's emotions and not add any additional stress.

I believe that if you are conducting yourself in a way that is truly making a positive difference in others' lives, you will leave a legacy that you can point to and enjoy while you're still alive.

By the way, do you think anyone from John's family will attend my funeral? I doubt they even remember my name or what I look like. But that's not the point. The point is, during a difficult time, I was extremely empathetic to what they were going through.

Do you believe the attitude I'm talking about can help in making your business more successful? More than you may know. Understanding how other people think and feel about things, i.e., empathy, is a necessary trait you should have if you're an entrepreneur.

"You can enjoy your legacy while you're still alive."

@realKevinCortez #EmbraceTheDetour

Everything I'm trying to convey on this topic is one of those things that cannot be taught. It must be caught.

Of course, there are principles to be learned, but if you do *not* naturally display such things as empathy, authenticity, humility, sincerity, and generosity from your heart, others will be able to sense that you're just pretending.

Once, when I was meeting with a potential client, they said, "Can I ask you a blunt question?"

I said, "Of course."

They said, "You keep giving me all these other options and pointing out how I could save money by doing some of your services myself or hiring someone else that would be less expensive. Do you not want me as a client?"

It caught me a bit off guard. And then I realized I was, in fact, doing that. She seemed surprised by my answer: "I want what's best for your business more than I want you as a client. I would love to do business with you, and I believe we could help you grow your company, but if you can be talked out of using our services by me or someone else, even if that someone is you, I think it's best to find that out before we proceed."

The truth is, I care more about what is best for people than simply creating a business transaction that somehow benefits me.

Consider what you are about to read very carefully: you will always leave money on the table by doing the right thing. But I believe the best way to conduct business is to try to make the right decision for everyone involved—always. I am totally committed to always having my client's best interest at heart.

P.S. That potential client did hire us for all her marketing needs.

A LIFE OF GIVING
As I mentioned, when I was running our family business, I was so grateful for the incredible support and counsel I

received from the various people who worked for our suppliers, e.g., Snapple, Coors, Red Bull, etc. I could simply pick up the phone and receive help on the different aspects of the business from someone who had big-time experience and really knew what they were talking about. You may also remember reading how I would ask myself on several occasions, "How in the world do small business owners make it without this kind of support?"

When I was a consultant, I became obsessed with providing that same type of help and support. Now, as a successful entrepreneur, nothing feels better than earning money on hard work, sweat, and tears—except, perhaps, giving back without expecting *anything* in return. It's hard for me to put this into business terms, but I genuinely believe that the more we give, good things have a way of happening in our lives. Doing good for other people is a great strategy.

Every couple of days, I find myself in a situation where I'm freely giving some of my best advice, the same advice for which people had paid over $325 an hour before. Some individuals are appreciative and end up wanting to integrate what I'm sharing into their business. Others don't place any value on what I'm showing them and simply discount my advice. This no longer bothers me because I know that doing the right thing always has a way of working out for me down the road in some unforeseen way.

Before I close out this chapter, I should mention that doing the right thing takes courage. These days, courage is in short supply. I know many people who are honest, have good intentions, and are kind, *but* they're parked on the side of the road. Why? Because they lack the courage to engage in the fight and actually do something that would make a difference.

If you are an entrepreneur, haven't you noticed it takes courage to keep driving forward when you find yourself in the middle of a detour on your journey? At times, everything within you wants to pull your car over and park so you won't have to deal with another unexpected challenge. But you know that the only way to get to where you need to be is to let your GPS reroute you, hold on, and then once again *#EmbraceTheDetour.*

Chapter Reflections

What are your thoughts? I would love for you to share some of your answers to these questions on any of my social media platforms. Go to "KevinCortez.com" and link to them from there.

1. Before reading this chapter, had you ever considered the difference between *inheritance* and *legacy*? In what ways are you leaving a legacy?

2. I make a big deal about investing myself in others. How important is it for you to give back to others?

3. As you consider the different ways you contribute to society, is there really anything that is holding you back from doing what you know you should be doing?

Scan the QR code for bonus content.

Final Word

It was New Year's Day, a day for making resolutions. Many people look forward to ringing in the New Year because they want to make a fresh start in their lives. As this particular New Year's Day was approaching, I definitely fit into that category, not so much because I was looking forward to the upcoming year, but because I could finally put the previous twelve months behind me. Have you ever had one of those years?

By all accounts, I was a business success. So, no one (including me) would have guessed I was on the brink of being emotionally overwhelmed. I was projecting strength and fearlessness, but my nerves had become completely shot.

Until recently, talking about your internal struggles was a sign of weakness. Rather than showing vulnerability, many entrepreneurs think they are supposed to come off as always having it all together. That is how I thought I should conduct myself … and I was wrong. Completely wrong.

On January 16, 2003, I experienced what I can only describe as a crisis of emotions. Basically, I flamed out. Until that day, I often found myself telling others who were feeling overwhelmed by their challenges:

"Never give up. Don't ever lose hope."

"When the going gets tough, the tough get going."

"When you feel like quitting, think about why you started."

"Blah, blah, blah."

Now I was the one burned out. I had allowed tremendous pressures to build up inside me over the years, and now I felt overwhelmed. I suddenly understood why people "snap" and do dumb stuff. When I received the typical hollow advice in my depressed state, I really had to suppress the urge to hit their baby toe with a hammer and tell them to "walk it off."

Over the years, I had become very focused (um, obsessed) when it came to how I approached life. A lot of what I had accomplished was through the sheer force of my self-effort and my strong determination. I was *sure* I would never encounter something I couldn't handle. I couldn't recall failing at anything significant.

Now, whatever you do, don't miss what I'm about to say: there is such a thing as willpower, but it can get you only so far, and then it will fail you miserably, every time. Have you ever wondered why some famous person, who seemed to have everything going for them, committed suicide? There may have been several reasons, but one thing's for sure: their self-centered willpower failed them on a major level.

According to researchers, many entrepreneurs share inborn character traits that make them more vulnerable to strong emotional states.[13] On the one hand, we can be very energetic, motivated, and creative. But on the other hand, those emotional states may also include depression, despair, hopelessness, worthlessness, loss of motivation, and suicidal thinking. That's why we should never be afraid to ask for help if we are experiencing symptoms of significant anxiety, stress, or depression.

As entrepreneurs, we must have a certain amount of ambition, passion, and drive, not to mention an unusual risk tolerance in order for us to take the chances we do and go after our entrepreneurial dreams. Those same passionate qualities of mind and character that drive us toward success can sometimes consume us if we are not careful.

And that's what happened to me.

When I look back at that period, I'm incredibly thankful I hit a wall because it forced me to find the balance necessary to be a truly happy person. I stopped striving so intensely for what everyone else held up as the subjective standard of success.

I began "doing life" in a way whereby the ebb and flow of living felt right to me. Finding the correct rhythm in life has made such a positive difference. I will *never* go back to how I was before. Now, don't get me wrong: I am still willing to go through seasons of working eighteen-hour days in order to "make things happen," but that is the rare exception, not the norm.

The Entrepreneur Detour will always be a wild ride, full of unexpected twists and turns, but there are adjustments we can make to help keep our lives from spiraling out of control. For me, what I found most important was to make time for my loved ones. I had let my business aspirations squeeze out my close relationships, and when it comes to staving off emotional distress, relationships with friends and family can be powerful weapons.

Another action I found extremely helpful was counting the costs of every decision I made. Everything has a price; know what it is.

I'm aware that many people don't want to accept the fact that *everything* has a price. They choose to believe that there is such a thing as a free lunch. And when they are confronted with the fact that *every action* exacts a price, they become unhappy, frustrated, or angry. Why? Because they don't want to pay what it costs. They would rather complain, act like a victim, and play the blame game.

While there are many different entrepreneurial traits, one characteristic is consistent: every successful entrepreneur has paid a price to be where they are at. Somewhere along their entrepreneurial journey, they determined they were willing to forgo certain things to have their own business. They knew nothing worth doing ever came easy. Nothing.

Here are four principles that have helped me count the cost in deciding what to pursue for my life and business:

1. *Accept* the fact that everything has a price.
2. *Determine* what the price is for what I'm wanting.
3. *Choose* whether I'm willing to pay the price or *choose* to go without.
4. *Don't complain* about the choice I made, and always be grateful for what I currently have.

To use my current business as an illustration, since I want to *level up* my company, most business leaders would advise me to begin hiring more employees to

THE ENTREPRENEUR DETOUR • 127

handle the growth. They would remind me that *growth* is the most important metric of an entrepreneur's success, and I should make sure to hire ahead of my expansion. But when I count the costs of hiring an employee, I know it goes way beyond a money-in/money-out decision. Employees change *everything* about your business.

Since I'm a small firm, if I hire a person who is not very productive, it could end up skyrocketing my company's operating costs. Realistically, since even a typically good employee only works at about *half* capacity, if I were to calculate the actual labor burden of that employee, I would most likely have to increase my revenue by six to ten times that person's salary to cover their actual expense.

Of course, it goes without saying that if I find the right person who is truly extraordinary and fits into our culture, the price of *not* hiring that A-player would be a far greater cost to my business than hiring them.

So, the question is not, "Do I want my business to grow tenfold?" Sure. It would be nice to have more revenue. But since I can't have the advantages of each choice, the question becomes, "Am I willing to pay the price, at this stage in my business, to increase sales so I can hire more employees?" Well, since the current profit of my business is acceptable to me, that's an easy-peasy answer: no thank you.

I just know myself. So, for *me*, the price of spending all my emotional energy trying to grow my agency's top-line revenue so I can pay for several employees, have a bit more cash in the bank, and tell everyone how big my company is, is too high. That's my position. And since I have accepted this fact, I'm super happy with where I am right now. And you will *never* find me complaining about it.

Actually, since we're on this subject, I am executing another plan that is moving Mobile Marketing Helper forward for growth. If you're interested in how I'm going about this, follow my progress at KevinCortez.com.

"Everything has a price; know what it is."

@realKevinCortez #EmbraceTheDetour

Once again, if you set out to make a change but don't count the cost, it's just a matter of time before the reality of the challenge will outstrip your desire to change. Count the cost, then make a move. Progress is always worth the price.

By the way, if you are the type of person who has determined you are willing to pay whatever the price is for what you are wanting, I deeply respect your decision. That's your choice. You need to "do you" and not worry about what anybody else (including me) thinks. Just make sure you have counted the costs and are okay with your decision.

What's the result or outcome you most want in your life right now? What is the price you would have to pay to experience that outcome? What change in your actions do you need to make to bring about your desired result? Now comes the time to act on the choice you've made.

Change can be tricky. But once you decide (for real) to change, your progress is set in motion. The good news is that your decision creates its own kind of momentum, and momentum rules the world. As your decision picks up momentum, it will carry you down the road.

Being an entrepreneur means facing uncertain challenges. They are the norm. But when we have momentum and encounter a detour, momentum says, "Hold on, not so fast. I'm still running things here, and we will keep going. If we turned left when we should have turned right, that's OK. We will simply not stop or give up until we're back on the road we need to be on."

Remember, it is *beyond amazing* what we entrepreneurs now have at our fingertips: Unbelievable production capabilities, with unlimited access to distribution on platforms like YouTube and Facebook, would have cost tens of millions of dollars in infrastructure just a couple of decades ago. Now, everybody's got a shot at entrepreneurship. Because of tech, there are no infrastructural or financial situations left that can stop anyone from choosing to pursue their entrepreneurial dream.

The Entrepreneur Detour is marked by action, followed by setbacks and failure, then more action. Moving forward can be the hardest part. Keep going and don't stop. The journey is your friend. Keep going.

One last thing: Love it or hate it, when you are done reading this book, I would like for you to let me know what you think.

I can't promise I will respond, but your chances of a response will certainly improve if you tell me how awesome you found all of this, and, more importantly, how you convinced all of your friends and fellow entrepreneurs that their lives will never be complete without reading this book.

And remember, *#EmbraceTheDetour*.

Your defender of all things entrepreneurial,

Kevin

P.S. It would mean the world to me if you took the time to write a review on Amazon. I would love to know what part spoke to you the most and if there is a topic you'd like to see me address in the future.

P.S.S. Be sure to check out how we can work together on the following page...

I've created something special just for the readers of this book. I've opened up my calendar so I can spend an entire day with you here in Dallas, addressing some of the critical needs of your business.

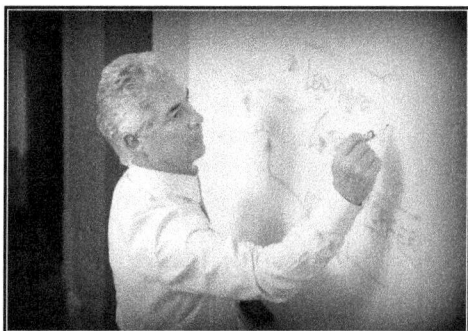

If you're interested in participating in this "Day in Dallas" program, then I want to invite you to apply with me personally. You can apply here:

Go to → Dallas.KevinCortez.com

After I receive your information, we'll give you a call and explain the program further to see if it's a good fit. If it is, we'll be spending a day together real soon.

ABOUT THE AUTHOR

Kevin Cortez, founder of *Kevin Cortez Media*, is an accomplished business owner, keynote speaker, and author. He has been featured in *Voyage Dallas Magazine* as one of "Dallas's most inspiring entrepreneurs!"

Kevin brings a level of business acumen to entrepreneurship that is rare in the emerging media landscape. Kevin's strong knowledge and understanding of business challenges, as well as marketing best practices, have helped grow revenue and increase bottom-line profits for several business owners.

Prior to starting his interactive marketing agency, Kevin had a twenty-five-year track record of business success, including leading his family's wholesale beverage distribution company in California for fifteen years, where it survived and overcame numerous challenges that threatened its overall existence and now enjoys a reputation as the largest beverage distributorship in its trading area.

During this time in California, Kevin was also the lead pastor of a non-denominational church for eleven years. While pastoring, Cortez wrote two Christian books that were distributed in over 30 countries.

MyGlobal.com

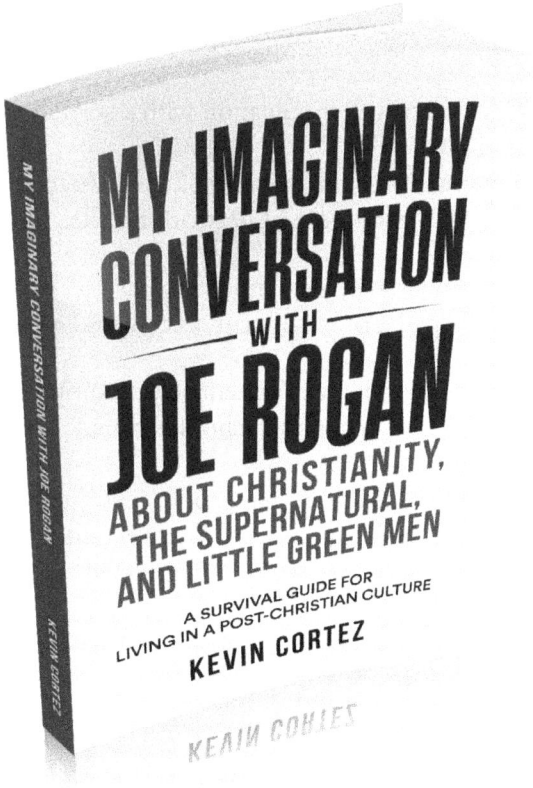

MY IMAGINARY CONVERSATION WITH — JOE ROGAN

ABOUT CHRISTIANITY, THE SUPERNATURAL, AND LITTLE GREEN MEN

A SURVIVAL GUIDE FOR LIVING IN A POST-CHRISTIAN CULTURE

KEVIN CORTEZ

available at
amazon

Notes

[1] Friedrich Nietzsche, *Twilight of the Idols*, (New York: Penguin Classics, 1990).

[2] "Percentage of U.S. population with a social media profile from 2008 to 2017," statista, https://www.statista.com/statistics/273476/percentage-of-us-population-with-a-social-network-profile.

[3] "Entrepreneurship," last modified July 16, 2017, https://en.wikipedia.org/wiki/Entrepreneurship.

[4] "EY transforms its recruitment selection process for graduates, undergraduates and school leavers," last modified August 3, 2015, http://www.ey.com/uk/en/newsroom/news-releases/15-08-03---ey-transforms-its-recruitment-selection-process-for-graduates-undergraduates-and-school-leavers.

[5] "The U.S. Beer Industry," America's Beer Distributors, https://www.nbwa.org/resources/industry-fast-facts.

[6] Ibid.

[7] Chriss W. Street, "California Wins 'Worst State to Do Business' for 11th Year," *Breitbart*, May 27, 2015, http://www.breitbart.com/big-government/2015/05/27/california-wins-worst-state-to-do-business-for-11th-year/.

[8] Chloe Albanesius, "Google's New Rule: Mobile First," *PCMag*, February 16, 2010, http://www.pcmag.com/article2/0,2817,2359752,00.asp

[9] Nicky Woolf, "Over 50 and once successful, jobless Americans seek support groups to help where Congress has failed," *The Guardian*, November 7, 2014, https://www.theguardian.com/money/2014/nov/07/lon g-term-unemployed-support-groups-congress

[10] Seth Godin, *Tribes: We Need You to Lead Us* (New York: Portfolio, 2008).

[11] "Elon Musk Tops Highest Paid CEO List," http://insideevs.com/elon-musk-tops-highest-paid-ceo-list

[12] Jenny Beth Martin, "OPINION: Can we wean Elon Musk off government support already?," *The Hill*, August 7, 2017, http://thehill.com/blogs/pundits-blog/economy-budget/345338-can-we-wean-elon-musk-off-government-support-already
Jerry Hirsch, "Elon Musk's growing empire is fueled by $4.9 billion in government subsidies," *Los Angeles Times*, May 30, 2015, http://www.latimes.com/business/la-fi-hy-musk-subsidies-20150531-story.html

[13] Jessica Bruder, "The Psychological Price of Entrepreneurship," *Inc.*, https://www.inc.com/magazine/201309/jessica-bruder/psychological-price-of-entrepreneurship.html

www.ingramcontent.com/pod-product-compliance
Lightning Source LLC
Chambersburg PA
CBHW060608200326
41521CB00007B/697